IMAGES
of America

BALTIMORE AND THE CIVIL RIGHTS MOVEMENT

IMAGES
of America

BALTIMORE AND THE CIVIL RIGHTS MOVEMENT

Philip Jackson Merrill
Foreword by Rev. Betty Jackson Merrill

ARCADIA
PUBLISHING

Published by Arcadia Publishing
Charleston, South Carolina

Printed in the United States of America

Library of Congress Control Number: 2023933049

For all general information, please contact Arcadia Publishing:
Telephone 843-853-2070
Fax 843-853-0044
E-mail sales@arcadiapublishing.com
For customer service and orders:
Toll-Free 1-888-313-2665

Visit us on the Internet at www.arcadiapublishing.com

To my life partner Veronica Asheia Carr, who has been the wind beneath my wings in this endeavor and all others.

CONTENTS

FOREWORD

The Civil Rights Movement was a formal political movement and campaign from 1954 to 1968 in the United States to abolish institutional racial segregation, discrimination, and disenfranchisement. But our struggle for civil rights began long before this time, and people and events in Baltimore were always front and center in the struggle.

This book highlights a wide variety of well-known and everyday civil rights activists and activities from the 1880s to the 1970s that shaped the civil rights of the city. Philip J. Merrill, my son, an African American historian, and the author of this book, said, unbeknownst to me, that I am an everyday civil rights activist because of my contributions to the struggle.

I was one of the first Black salespersons at the Hecht Company in downtown Baltimore; was in the first three classes that integrated Western High School; was an exchange teacher at the all-white Leithwalk Elementary School; belonged to the first Black family to integrate the historic Ten Hills community; was a partner in an interracial marriage, which lasted for 44 years and began in 1968, the first year miscegenation was not outlawed in Baltimore; was a special assistant to the first Black public school system superintendent; was a ranking Black professional at the Baltimore Gas and Electric Company; and cofounded with her husband Interrace, an organization dedicated to educating others about interracial couples and children. Chapters were in Baltimore City, Baltimore County, Howard County, and Harford County, Maryland.

Philip said that if it were not for the thousands of everyday activists like me, the struggle would be more than what it still is today.

If anyone would know who these activists and activities were, it is Philip. He is truly a phenomenal African American historian with an exceptional ability to ferret out our artifacts, connect their dots, and tell authentic and largely unknown stories.

I am so blessed that he has dedicated his life to his never-ending artifactual journey to the benefit of our country's history. And I am especially honored to be a part of the journey.

—Rev. Betty Jackson Merrill

ACKNOWLEDGMENTS

First and foremost, I thank God for planting the seed for this project and rendering unto me an unparalleled archive that provided everything needed to complete it.

Also, it is with sincere gratitude that I thank my loved ones, starting with my great-grandmother Gertrude B. Jackson, also known as "Nanny Jack" in her historic Sandtown neighborhood of Old West Baltimore. She was the inspiration for my love of history, and it was from her that I learned to value and collect the wisdom of age and the stories of artifacts, people, and things around me. I also thank my late father, Rev. George B. Merrill, who speaks to me and encourages me daily to continue my work; my mother, Rev. Betty L. Merrill, my first teacher and inspirational guide; my life partner and the digital media strategist for Nanny Jack & Co, LLC, Veronica A. Carr, whose tireless work ethic and dedication in helping me preserve the Nanny Jack & Co. Archives is unmatched; my daughters, Indie Rose and Isabella Louise Carr Merrill, who inspire me; my uncles Martin L. Jackson and John H. Brooks; my relatives Bob Jones and Jacqueline Foote; and my faithful lifelong friend Ricky Boots.

In addition, I sincerely thank the following individuals who have contributed their stories, assistance, and research efforts: Marion McGaskey Blackwell, founder of Urban Lites. LLC; Alex and Joan Brown; Monica Pinkett; Dr. Alyssa Sommers, PharmD; Richard McKoy; Diane Bell-McKoy, founder of Opportunity Connection, LLC; retired judge Robert M. Bell; Patricia Waddy; Eva Slezak, longtime specialist at the Enoch Pratt Free Library; Greg French Early Photography; Dr. Donna T. Hollie, PhD, of Heritage Associates; Courtney Wilson; Paul Roeger; Ronald and Marianne Kreitner; Bill Jessup; Wayne Gilreath; and Clint Hall, owner of Create A Video in Mint Hill, North Carolina.

A tremendous debt of gratitude to Caitrin Cunningham, the senior title manager at Arcadia Publishing, who consistently exhibited the utmost patience, helpfulness, and guidance in bringing this book to fruition.

Lastly, thanks to these three venerable institutions for invaluable research: the Maryland State Archives, the *Afro-American* newspaper, and the Enoch Pratt Free Library. I am also grateful for the genealogical services of ancestry.com.

All images appear courtesy of Nanny Jack & Co. Archives.

INTRODUCTION

"We must ensure that Black history is told fully and accurately in America. While the truth of our journey may not be the easiest to tell, it should be protected and celebrated, because the story of African American people is intricate and integral to the story of the United States of America—that history must be treated and admired as such."

These words were spoken by Rep. Kweisi Mfume as he announced the introduction of his National Council on African American History and Culture Act of 2023.

Mfume's words embody the goal of this book—to tell the full and accurate narrative of Baltimore's decades-long civil rights movement. As Maryland's largest city, Baltimore made major contributions to the nation's struggle for freedom, equality, and opportunity. However, it has been largely overlooked in the overall Civil Rights Movement. Today's larger public generally thinks of the movement that lasted from 1954 to 1968 in the South with the Montgomery, Alabama, bus boycotts; Rev. Dr. Martin Luther King Jr.'s rousing speeches and marches; the "I Am A Man" sanitation workers strike in Memphis, Tennessee; or the Greensboro, North Carolina, sit-ins at the infamous Woolworth's lunch counter. But there is so much more, particularly when it comes to the Baltimore story.

According to the Oxford English Dictionary, civil rights are defined as the rights of every citizen to political and social freedom and equality. While this definition may seem simple, it has not always been realized for Black Americans, and particularly for Black Baltimoreans. This book covers the civil rights struggle in the 1890s and continues through the 1900s, encompassing the events after the 1968 riots brought on by the assassination of Dr. King.

In the 1890s, Baltimore was a thriving seaport city with a population of over 430,000, up from 330,000 in 1880. Its substantial maritime trades and manufacturing industry contributed to this population boom as Blacks from the South, other Maryland regions, and European immigrants flocked to the city to work in factories and plants such as Sparrows Point, Bethlehem Steel, and the F.S. Royster Guano Company. The Blacks and European migrants created a greater demand for new housing in an already crowded city. However, the city enacted residential segregation ordinances, restricting Blacks from moving into white neighborhoods because of fears of race-mixing.

Educational opportunities were limited for Black children. In response, the Mutual United Brotherhood of Liberty, along with numerous Black churches, fraternal orders, benevolent societies, and other civic organizations, formed their own schools. The Mutual Brotherhood also advocated that the schools be overseen by members of their own race, which led to the appointment of the first Black teachers and principals to Black schools.

As the Monumental City entered the 20th century, the fight for civil rights intensified as Baltimore tightened its grip on Black rights. Black citizens were barred from attending certain colleges and universities and could not eat in certain establishments, and white residents widened the boundary of where Blacks could not live. Black lawyers could not join the long-standing law associations, and Black doctors could not practice at Johns Hopkins Hospital, one of the nation's premier medical facilities.

The Niagara Movement, modeled after the Mutual United Brotherhood of Liberty, was created in 1905 to address these and other issues faced by the nation's Black population. Baltimoreans such as the Revs. James Robert Lincoln Diggs and Garnett Russell Waller Sr. were among the group's founders. However, as membership and funding dwindled, the Niagara Movement paved the path for a new organization: the National Association for the Advancement of Colored People (NAACP), which began in 1909.

In 1912, the Baltimore chapter of the NAACP was formed, making it the second-oldest branch in the country. The Baltimore NAACP fought against disenfranchisement bills, housing segregation, limited educational opportunities, and employment discrimination. It instigated the nation's first lawsuit against residential housing segregation in 1938 with *Meade v. Dennistone* and sparked a series of nationwide sit-ins at segregated restaurants, beginning with the 1955 sit-ins at Read's Drug Store in downtown Baltimore.

However, the NAACP was not the only organization active in the movement. The Baltimore Urban League, Frontiers Club, the Baltimore chapter of the National Association of Colored Women, Sharp Street Memorial United Methodist Church, Morgan State University, Coppin State University, the Maryland Commission on Interracial Relations, and countless others held mass meetings, established voter registration drives, and encouraged political activism.

While influential civil rights figures such as the Mitchell family, the Jackson family, and Thurgood Marshall are often celebrated as the face of Baltimore's civil rights movement, there were so many others who made their marks. Revs. Harvey E. Johnson, William M. Alexander, William A. Creditt, and the other members of the Mutual United Brotherhood of Liberty fought against Jim Crow laws by establishing schools and advocating for the right of Blacks to practice law in Maryland. The editors of the venerable *Afro-American Ledger* urged readers to vote against laws that sought to take away their rights to vote and purchase property and provided a voice for the rising Black community.

Attorneys like William Ashbie Hawkins turned to the courts to fight discrimination. Hawkins, an early Black student at the University of Maryland School of Law, was expelled when the school was resegregated. He completed his law degree at Howard University and was admitted to the Maryland Bar in 1897. He partnered with George W.F. McMechen, and they formed the nationally recognized law firm Hawkins and McMechen. They argued several eminent cases, including the 1917 Supreme Court case *Buchanan v. Worley*, which revolved around segregation ordinances. In the 1920s, Hawkins entered the political arena with his newly formed Independent Republican League that included some of the city's top Black doctors, attorneys, entrepreneurs, and suffragettes on his campaign committee. He unsuccessfully ran for the US Senate, but his pioneering campaign inspired other Blacks who eventually occupied seats in the Baltimore City Council, Maryland General Assembly, and Maryland State Senate.

Black Baltimoreans always found ways to excel despite the state's attempts to suppress them. A long-standing state law barred Black residents from attending white public universities and relegated them to the four Black colleges, which did not offer graduate or professional programs. In order to get master's degrees and PhDs, numerous Black students attended the University of Pennsylvania, Columbia University in New York, or New York University, to name a few. Many of them received advanced degrees in education and returned to teach in Baltimore's segregated school system. Generations of students benefited from highly qualified educators who taught English, mathematics, French, and a variety of other subjects. It was not until 1936 that one white university, the University of Maryland School of Law, was integrated, and others soon followed.

All of these efforts culminated decades later with two monumental events: the 1963 March on Washington and the 1964 Civil Rights Act. In both instances, Black Baltimoreans were front and center. Ministers, lawyers, activists, and community leaders met at churches, schools, the colored YMCA, and Sharp Street Community House to encourage citizens to join the march on the National Mall in nearby Washington, DC. The influx of Black Baltimoreans added to the more than 200,000 attendees in Washington on August 28, 1963. A year later, another Baltimorean made history for his role in the passage of civil rights legislation. Clarence M. Mitchell Jr. was an NAACP lobbyist who became known as the "101st US Senator" due to his efforts to get Pres.

Lyndon B. Johnson to sign the 1964 Civil Rights Act. The bill was the most progressive in almost a century; it prohibited discrimination in public places, officially ended school segregation, and made employment discrimination illegal. The years 2023 and 2024 will mark the 60th anniversaries for these important milestones and will bring renewed interest and scholarship to these events.

As a native son of historic Old West Baltimore, I witnessed the city's civil rights journey. In April 1968, days after the assassination of Rev. Dr. Martin Luther King Jr., I remember the feelings of fear, as a young child, when the National Guard was brought in to quell the violence in my immediate neighborhood and surrounding streets. It left an indelible mark on me, and I can still vividly recall it as if it were yesterday. My immediate family also participated in various civil rights activities that I grew up hearing about.

For that reason, I felt compelled to write about Baltimore's tremendous civil rights journey because it holds a rich history and legacy, and there are many stories to tell about every community within the city. The city's civil rights journey not only had an impact on Baltimore but also the region and nation.

I hope this book will introduce readers to the lesser known individuals and activities of Baltimore's civil rights movements that tell its story. I also hope it will help them to recognize the level of urgency as many of the older civil rights pioneers are transitioning, which makes it more important to gather information and acknowledge their involvement.

While this book is a celebration of those who laid the groundwork for the modern Civil Rights Movement, it is also a stark reminder of all the work we still have to do. Whether you record oral history, write articles highlighting activists, or advocate for civil rights legislation, we all have a role to play in honoring our ancestors and carrying on the work they began almost two centuries ago.

Throughout the book, there will be references to the former names of Morgan State University, Coppin State University, and the *AFRO*. For purposes of clarification, here is a brief timeline of each institution's name changes.

MORGAN STATE UNIVERSITY was founded in 1867 as the Centenary Biblical Institute and was known by this name until 1890. The institution was then named Morgan College, until 1939, when the name was changed to Morgan State College. The college kept this name until 1975, when they changed to their present name, Morgan State University.

COPPIN STATE UNIVERSITY. In 1901, Baltimore City Board of Education initiated a one-year course for training Black elementary school teachers at what was known as the Colored High and Training School, at Dolphin Street and Pennsylvania Avenue. In 1902, the program expanded to become a two-year Normal Department within the school. In 1909, it became an institution separate from the high school with its own principal, moving to Mount and Saratoga Streets. In 1926, it was renamed Fanny Jackson Coppin Normal School in honor of the pioneering educator. By 1938, the curriculum had expanded to four years and the name was changed to Coppin Teachers College. In 1950, it became a part of Maryland's higher education system and was renamed Coppin State Teachers College. In 1952, the college moved to its current site on West North Avenue, renamed Coppin State College in 1967, and Coppin State University, its present name, in 2004.

The *AFRO AMERICAN LEDGER* was founded in 1892 as a merger of three different publications: Murphy's *The Sunday School Helper*; *The Afro-American*, owned by Rev. William Moncure Alexander; and *The Ledger*, owned by Rev. George Freeman Bragg Jr. The newspaper changed its name in 1917 to the *Afro American Newspaper,* and today it is simply known as the *AFRO*.

One

THE PROGRESSIVE ERA
1890–1920

Due to its large free Black antebellum population that laid the groundwork, the city of Baltimore was primed for various civil rights activities. This community of successful churches, businesses, publishers, and benevolent societies pushed for equal rights in all aspects of life, from education and transportation to employment and voting rights. After the passage of the 15th Amendment in 1870, which granted voting rights to African American men, Black Baltimoreans mobilized to fight for additional rights.

With the emergence of the impactful civil rights organization the Mutual United Brotherhood of Liberty, Black Baltimoreans had a strong advocate on the forefront of the movement. This group was led by a combination of formerly enslaved and freeborn ministers and community leaders who set the tone for activism leading into the 20th century.

At the beginning of the 20th century, newly established lawyers, doctors, and educational leaders continued the fight in courtrooms, classrooms, communities, and city hall. These activities culminated in the formation of the National Association for the Advancement of Colored People (NAACP) in 1909 and its Baltimore branch in 1912.

Peter Paul Brown founded the Ancient United Order of Sons and Daughters, Brothers and Sisters of Moses, an African American fraternal organization, in 1867. Brown, who was a mariner and a practicing physician, lived in Baltimore's Fells Point community for a number of years at the Seaman's Boarding House. Blacks were excluded from joining white fraternal orders, so Brown formed the group to offer death benefits, healthcare, and fellowship during the Reconstruction era.

The Ancient United Order of Sons and Daughters, Brothers and Sisters of Moses, had chapters around the country, including this one at 608 North Eutaw Street in Baltimore. Solomon A. Bond (seated fourth from the left in the first row) was the Grand Master of the order. He spearheaded an effort in the early 1900s to celebrate Peter Paul Brown Day in honor of the order's founder.

Educational opportunities for Black Baltimoreans were limited in the mid 1800s. However, churches, fraternal orders, and benevolent societies formed their own schools and welcomed students of all backgrounds—formerly enslaved or freeborn, young and old. The Ancient United Order of Sons and Daughters, Brothers and Sisters of Moses, often provided financial support or a building to house the school, like this one from the early 1900s.

Rev. Wesley J. Parker was one of the first African American trustees of the Centenary Biblical Institute (now Morgan State University). Until Reverend Parker became a trustee in 1872, the board was made up of white philanthropists, educators, and community leaders who made decisions about the institute's funding, chose teachers, and decided what would be taught. Having African American trustees allowed the Black community to make decisions in the best interest of the institution and its students.

Rev. Dr. Harvey Elijah Johnson, the formerly enslaved pastor of Union Baptist Church, was a civil rights leader who cofounded the Mutual United Brotherhood of Liberty in 1885. This organization was an earlier iteration of the Niagara Movement, which eventually became the National Association for the Advancement of Colored People. Johnson and the Brotherhood fought to get Black teachers and principals into Black schools at a time when Baltimore had barred them.

Amelia Etta Hall Johnson was a Canadian-born writer, poet, and the wife of Rev. Dr. Harvey Elijah Johnson. She was the first woman and first African American to be published by the American Baptist Publication Society, one of the largest publishing houses in the country. Many of Johnson's nonfiction works echoed the call by Black leaders for African Americans to be self-sufficient and establish their own institutions separate from the control of white society.

Rev. William Moncure Alexander was the pastor of Sharon Baptist Church and served as vice president of the Mutual United Brotherhood of Liberty. He also chaired the organization's education committee, which called for the hiring of Black teachers, expansion of the Colored High School curriculum from two to four years, increase in the number of primary and grammar schools for Black children, and improvements in the condition of Black schools. The William M. Alexander Elementary School No. 112, Laurens and Calhoun Streets, was named for him.

Rev. Dr. William Abraham Creditt was a general agent for the Mutual United Brotherhood of Liberty, a civil rights organization that preceded the Niagara Movement. He pastored several Baptist churches, including Leadenhall Baptist Church. In 1889, Creditt solicited donations for the Black men accused in the Navassa Island incident. The men were accused of shooting white supervisors at a Caribbean Island phosphate company and were brought to Baltimore for trial.

15

In 1889, Fannie L. Barbour became the first Black woman principal of a colored Baltimore school. This was made possible by the efforts of the Mutual United Brotherhood of Liberty, particularly their education committee. Barbour spent over 40 years in the Baltimore school system and inspired many of her students to enter the educational field. In 1950, a Baltimore elementary school was named for her.

Rev. Peter Carter Neal was one of the leading pastors of several Baptist churches in Baltimore, including First Baptist Church. In 1889, he organized and served as the first president of the Colored YMCA of Baltimore when it was located at Calvert and Centre Streets. Reverend Neal was also instrumental in the establishment of Dunbar Junior High School in East Baltimore.

This rare 1902 photograph features prominent AME bishops and ministers and their wives in Cape Town, South Africa. Bishop Benjamin Tucker Tanner (first row, third from left) pastored Bethel AME Church, where he advocated for quality educational opportunities for Blacks. Others in the picture include Rev. William Sampson Brooks (first row, fourth from left), who became a bishop in 1920 and was an early 1890s graduate of the Centenary Biblical Institute (now Morgan State University). Bishop James Anderson Handy (next to Brooks) founded Payne AME Church and published *Scraps of African Methodist Episcopal History* in 1902, a critical publication that gave an overview of the history of the AME church and its ministers and bishops. Bishop Levi Jenkins Coppin (first row, far right) pastored Bethel AME Church from 1881 to 1883, during which time he was appointed as the editor of the *AME Church Review*, which highlighted political, religious, and significant social issues. His wife, Fannie Jackson Coppin (second from right) was a formerly enslaved educator, missionary, and advocate for higher education for Black women. Coppin State University is named for her.

In this 1905 photograph are William Dean Pickens (second from left), George W.F. McMechen (third from left), William Ashbie Hawkins (fourth from left), Rev. James Robert Lincoln Diggs (first on the left), and a number of unidentified men. Hawkins and McMechen were prominent attorneys and activists; Pickens was an educator, author, and activist; and Diggs was a minister, activist, and the first African American in the nation to receive a doctorate in sociology.

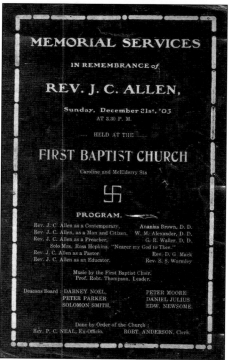

This December 31, 1905, program memorialized Rev. John Calvin Allen, the deceased pastor of First Baptist Church. During his life, Allen pastored several Baptist churches in Baltimore, including Leadenhall Baptist Church. Early in his career, Allen encouraged his parishioners to not only vote but to support independent candidates, whom he believed had in mind the best interests of the Black population.

This rare 1909 Colored High School football team photograph includes several pioneers who established basketball for young Black men in Baltimore's colored school system in 1907: Walter T. Webb (second row, third from the left), Leonard Ulysses Gibson (second row, fourth from the left), and Milton Q. Dorsey (third row standing, fourth from left). This was the beginning of removing the racial barriers placed on African Americans in sports.

Joseph Dorsey was the founder and publisher of the *Crusader*, a newspaper for Baltimore's Black community. Dorsey used the newspaper to discuss his views on several issues that affected the Black community, including their longstanding loyalty to the Republican party. In 1921, Dorsey wrote that thousands of Black Baltimoreans were disgusted with the failed promises of equal rights by the Republicans and should switch their affiliation to the Democratic Party.

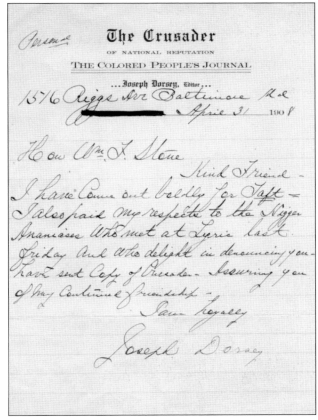

Booker Taliaferro Washington was a formerly enslaved author, orator, adviser to several US presidents, and the first president of Tuskegee Normal and Industrial Institute, now known as Tuskegee University. In this March 28, 1910, letter to John H. Murphy Sr., the formerly enslaved publisher of the *Afro-American Ledger* (now known as the *Afro*), Washington thanked Murphy for including an appeal for funds for Tuskegee Institute in the newspaper. The newspaper was not only a vehicle for supporting African American educational institutions, like Tuskegee, but also for shedding light on the financial difficulties faced by these institutions.

BOOKER T. WASHINGTON
TUSKEGEE INSTITUTE, ALABAMA
March 28, 1910

Personal

Mr. J. H. Murphy,

c/o Afro-American Ledger, Baltimore, Md.

My dear Mr. Murphy:-

Permit me to thank you most heartily for the generous manner in which you treated the appeal for endowment for Tuskegee. It was very kind of you to display it in the way that you did on your front page.

I hope at some time I will be in a position to repay you for some of your many and constant acts of kindness.

Yours very truly,

H

Rev. Daniel Grafton Hill Sr. (seated in the middle) was the pastor of Bethel AME Church. This photograph was taken at the church's former Saratoga Street location, where the church remained until 1911. During Hill's pastorate, his congregation organized campaigns to prevent the passage of several disenfranchisement bills, including the 1904 Poe Amendment. In 1908, Hill delivered a sermon against the Straus Amendment, which required Black men to own property in order to vote.

Martha Howard Murphy was the wife of *Afro-American Ledger* founder John Henry Murphy Sr. and the cofounder of the Colored Young Women's Christian Association. She served as president of the Baltimore branch at 1200 Druid Hill Avenue for 17 years. In 1892, she loaned her husband $200 to start the *Afro-American Ledger*, now known as the *Afro-American Newspaper*. In the early 1900s, Murphy and a number of other women organized the Women of Baltimore Against the Disenfranchisement Amendment.

ORIGINAL · FOWLER · STUDIO

238 N. Eighth St. Philadelphia

William Edward Burghardt "W.E.B." Du Bois was a sociologist, activist, author, editor, and cofounder of the National Association for the Advancement of Colored People (NAACP). In April 1912, Du Bois delivered a speech before the first public meeting of the Baltimore branch of the NAACP at the historic Union Baptist Church. He praised the work of the NAACP but urged African Americans to demand every right they deserved as American citizens.

Lucy Diggs Slowe, pioneering women's tennis champion and longtime dean of women at Howard University in Washington, DC, served as the secretary for the Baltimore NAACP in 1913. She used her platform to champion Black women in the suffrage movement. She was a graduate of the city's Colored High School (later renamed Frederick Douglass High School) and returned to Baltimore after graduating from Howard University and taught at her alma mater.

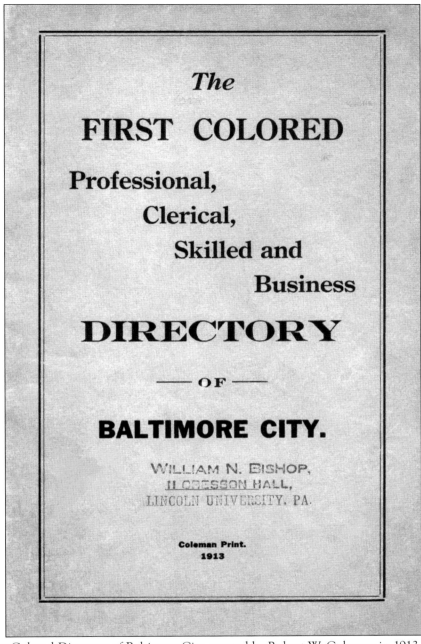

The

FIRST COLORED

Professional,

Clerical,

Skilled and

Business

DIRECTORY

—— OF ——

BALTIMORE CITY.

WILLIAM N. BISHOP,
11 CRESSON HALL,
LINCOLN UNIVERSITY, PA.

Coleman Print.
1913

The First Colored Directory of Baltimore City, created by Robert W. Coleman in 1913, featured advertisements for Black businesses and offered biographical sketches of prominent citizens. Although Coleman was blind by 1912, he did not let this deter him. With help from his wife, Mary, and their six daughters, he published the directory until 1946. He also advocated for blind and handicapped children and adults. In October 1913, he established the Maryland Association for the Colored Blind, which improved health services for blind Black children and adults. In 1925, he created the Association for the Handicapped, which offered services for Black handicapped children, such as transportation to school.

Come and go with us on our
...First Grand Moonlight...
OF THE SEASON
TO GREATER BROWN'S GROVE
Given by the "JOHN ALBERT CLUB"
Of Baltimore and Washington
Tuesday Evening, -:- June 24th, 1913
Music by Prof. Bell's Orchestra
TICKETS, - 25 CENTS
Steamer Starlight leaves Miller's Wharf at 8 sharp

Greater Brown's Grove was established by Capt. George W. Brown in the early 1900s as a resort for African Americans that featured refreshments, rides, and music. It offered Black organizations, schools, churches, and individuals an opportunity to enjoy the waterfront without fear of discrimination. During this era, many steamers operated by white companies either restricted Blacks to a certain section of the ship or banned them entirely. The *Afro-American Ledger* published a weekly list of who was going to Brown's Grove. Pictured here are a rare June 1913 ticket from the John Albert Club's midnight outing and a vernacular image of two women at Brown's Grove in the summer of 1918.

The Druid Hill Avenue Colored YMCA opened in 1911 at 1619 Druid Hill Avenue. However, the idea of a colored YMCA began in 1893 with the Mutual United Brotherhood of Liberty, which petitioned the central YMCA, then located at Pierce and Schroeder Streets, to create the Colored YMCA of Baltimore. The building offered a space to hold religious, fraternal, and club meetings; sports activities for children, and lodging for single Black men who were denied lodging at white establishments.

This page is from the 1914 ledger of the historic Trinity Baptist Church, founded in June 1888, which was an integral part of Baltimore's early civil rights movement. The church's first pastor, Rev. Garnett Russell Waller Sr., was one of the founders of the Niagara Movement, which ultimately became the NAACP. Waller also served as the first president of the Baltimore branch of the NAACP when it was established in 1912.

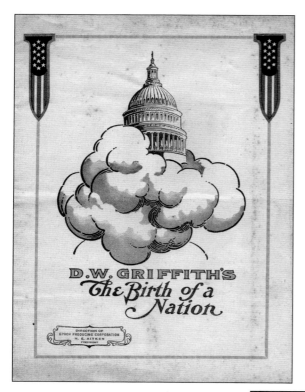

The Birth of a Nation, D.W. Griffith's film based on the novel *The Klansman*, premiered at Baltimore's Ford Theatre on March 6, 1916. The film demonized African American men by portraying them as sexual deviants who preyed on white women and ridiculed white politicians who had voted for rights for African Americans. This drew outrage from reporters at the *Afro-American Ledger*, who worked closely with the national NAACP to restrict the film's distribution.

Mary Burnett Talbert was an orator, activist, suffragist and one of the founders of the Niagara Movement, the precursor to the NAACP. In August 1916, Talbert was in Baltimore for the annual convention of the National Association of Colored Women. She spoke about the need for passage of a suffrage bill that would grant all women the right to vote.

The National Equal Rights League was founded in Syracuse, New York, in 1864 and was one of the oldest civil rights organizations in the country. Rev. Dr. James Robert Lincoln Diggs, the pastor who succeeded Rev. Garnett Russell Waller Sr. at Trinity Baptist Church, served as the organization's vice president. The organization fought to end lynching and advocated for Black women's voting rights, education, and employment opportunities. When the group dissolved, many members then joined the NAACP, and Diggs served as an early president of the Baltimore branch. This 1933 memorial offering envelope honored Reverend Diggs, who had been deceased for 10 years.

TEN "**Memorial Offering**" YEARS

"Blessed are the dead which die in the Lord, from henceforth, Yea, saith the Spirit, that they may rest from their labors; and their works do follow them."—REV. 14:13.

1923 Tenth Anniversary Memorial **1933**
——FOR THE LATE——

Rev. Jas. R. L. Diggs, A. B., A. M., Ph. D.

Former Pastor of Trinity Baptist Church, Baltimore, Maryland

SUNDAY MAY 28, 1933 AT 3 P. M.

(Please give ten cents for each year.)

NAME .... AMOUNT ....

REV. V. V. K. STOKES, Pastor.   W. H. JACKSON, Church Clerk

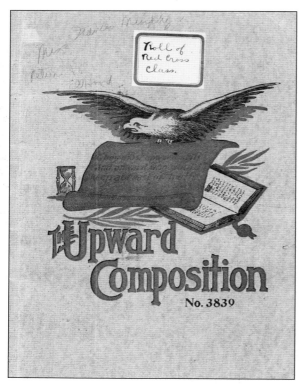

Although African Americans were not restricted from joining the Red Cross, services were often segregated, and whites were given preference. This extended to Black soldiers, who were often denied basic comforts. Frances L. Murphy, daughter of *Afro-American Ledger* founder John Henry Murphy Sr., organized a Red Cross drive to raise money for Black soldiers. This page from the Red Cross roll book lists students from the Colored High School (now Frederick Douglass High School); the Colored Training School (now Coppin State University); Morgan College (now Morgan State University); and several churches—including Bethel AME Church, Trinity Baptist Church, and Sharp Street Memorial Methodist Church who donated money and supplies, including candy and hand-knitted scarves and socks.

From Morgan College

1. Greta Johns
2. Ellen Mills
3. Mary Wilson
4. Frances Banks
5. Georgia Lawrence
6. Manila Crews
7. Inez Kelly
8. Fannie Madison Needles
9. Beulah Dorsey
10. Ethel Waters
11. Gladys Wilson
12. Bessie Bearers
13. Mary Watkins
    Diggs   From Colored Training School.
14. Miss E.R. Brown + Katherine Oliver
15. " Cecelia Connor
16. " Agnes Mills   (Work being returned thru
17. " Camper   (Miss Murphy
18. " Henderson
19. " Anderson
20. " Hattie Hicks
21. " Ruth Taylor.
        Eulalia Weingust
        Fannie Glascoe
        Lillian Francis

The *Afro-American* newspaper played a vital role in reporting on Black soldiers in World War I. The newspaper shared the experiences of soldiers through letters sent to family members or Frances L. Murphy (pictured below), the daughter of *Afro-American Ledger* founder John Henry Murphy Sr. In this April 1919 letter from Pvt. Jerome Briscoe, he thanked Murphy for the copy of the *Afro* that she had sent and mentioned how the Black soldiers "fight for a chance" to read it. The *Afro*, like many other Black publications of the era, provided an accurate interpretation of Black soldiers and their struggles and triumphs during the war.

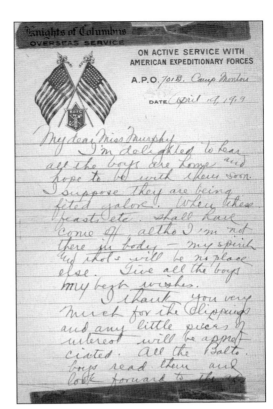

William Ashbie Hawkins was one of Baltimore's first Black lawyers. Over the course of his storied career, he represented numerous clients in civil rights cases involving lynching, housing segregation, and transportation. He had one of the nation's most recognizable law firms with his partner and brother-in-law George W.F. McMechen. In 1920, Hawkins was the first African American to run for Maryland State Senate with his recently formed Independent Republican League.

The Maryland Baptist Home for Aged Colored People was created in 1920 at 1620 West Lexington Street and is the oldest Black-owned and -operated nursing home in Maryland. It was managed by the United Baptist Missionary Convention of Maryland. The home filled a void for many elderly Blacks who might have struggled to find adequate housing, including those who were formerly enslaved.

The Monumental Lodge of Elks was located at 414 West Hoffman Street, which is the address to which the lodge moved in 1907. The lodge counted among its members several civil rights activists, including George W.F. McMechen, Truly Hatchett, Roy S. Bond, and Dr. Charles H. Fowler. The lodge, which had local, regional, and national affiliations, worked closely with churches to provide shelter, support, and money to civil rights organizations.

Truly Hatchett, real estate dealer and insurance broker, was one of the first two African Americans elected to the Maryland State House of Delegates. Hatchett used his position to encourage other African Americans to run for political office. During the 1920s, Hatchett improved the availability of housing for African Americans during Jim Crow. He was also the Exalted Ruler of Monumental Lodge No. 3 of the Improved Benevolent and Protective Order of Elks of the World.

IN TESTIMONY WHEREOF, the said parties have hereunto subscribed their names and affixed their seals the day and year first above written.

Test:

Carlos C Jennings

The Banneker Building Co. of Balto. City
By W. Ashbie Hawkins, Presd (SEAL)

W. Norman Bishop (SEAL)

(SEAL)

The Banneker Building at 14 East Pleasant Street, a four-story complex, opened in June 1920. It appears to be the first structure owned and operated by Black lawyers in Baltimore. It was located in the city's business district and within walking distance of the courthouse. Attorney William Ashbie Hawkins and his law partner and brother-in-law George W.F. McMechen practiced in the building; Hawkins served as the president of the Banneker Building Company, and McMechen served as the company's secretary. Attorney Clarke L. Smith served as the manager, and William C. McCard was the treasurer. The landlord and tenant agreement pictured here was signed by Hawkins, who leased office space to attorney William Norman Bishop, and Notary Public Carlos C. Jennings, who was associated with the law offices of William C. McCard. Many civil rights cases were handled by the various attorneys affiliated with this address.

Two

THE ROARING TWENTIES
1921–1929

During the Roaring Twenties, Baltimore, also known as the Monumental City, was in a state of change. In addition to the influx of Blacks from the South, the city was also preparing for the return of Black World War I soldiers. Black political power expanded with the election of attorneys Warner T. McGuinn and William L. Fitzgerald to the Baltimore City Council, where issues such as voting rights, education, employment, and housing were advanced. In 1924, Lillian Lottier was elected as the first female president of the Baltimore NAACP, where she spearheaded efforts to increase membership, launched voter registration drives, and fought to end discrimination in employment. This aided in the construction of the city's first high school built solely for Black students in Baltimore in 1924, Frederick Douglass High School, named in honor of the formerly enslaved abolitionist, orator, and author. The school produced numerous civil rights leaders during the decade, notably Thurgood Marshall and William I. Gosnell, who would put the country on a fast track to integration and equality in the coming years.

This decade also saw the formation of the Baltimore Urban League, an organization dedicated to helping Blacks achieve equality in education, employment, healthcare, and housing. Two pioneering housing developments, Wilson Park and Morgan Park, continued to offer single dwelling detached homes with land to those who wished to live in a less congested environment. Two major structures for Blacks, one for entertainment and the other for lawyers, were built during this time. The Douglass Theatre was incorporated in 1922 and offered Black audiences an opportunity to be entertained in a space that was owned by their race. The Banneker Law Building, in Baltimore's business district, housed some of the city's most noteworthy civil rights attorneys.

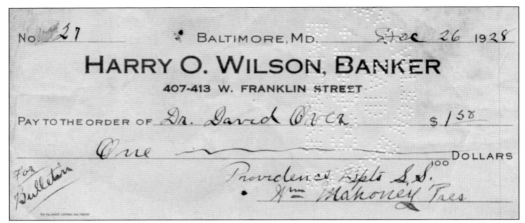

The Harry O. Wilson Bank was founded by Black businessman, real estate developer, and philanthropist Harry O'Neill Wilson Sr. The bank was one of the first to provide loans for Blacks to purchase homes and build churches and institutions. Wilson's bank was one of 15 Black banks across the United States that survived the Great Depression. This December 26, 1928, check for $1 was made out to Dr. David E. Over, the pastor of Providence Baptist Church.

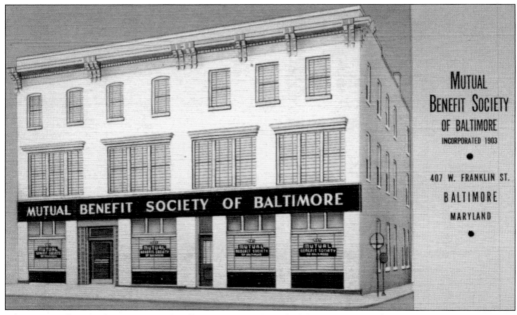

The Mutual Benefit Society of Baltimore was founded by Harry O. Wilson Sr. in 1903 at the northeast corner of Pearl and Fayette Streets. By 1920, it had relocated to 407–413 West Franklin Street. The organization provided sick, death, and health insurance for Blacks. During this era, Black Baltimoreans were often denied health and death benefits from white insurance companies or charged unreasonably high fees. The company employed hundreds of Black Baltimoreans for over 70 years.

The Free Summer Excursion Society of Baltimore was founded by white philanthropist John T. Ford in 1871 to provide country outings for mothers and children. The group reflected the segregation of the city; certain Thursdays were for Black mothers and children. The female members of the organization walked through neighborhoods and handed out tickets, like this one for an excursion held in August 1921, which provided for round-trip boat fare to a country beach resort and lunch.

The Sharp Street Community House at 1206 Etting Street was designed by Black architect Arthur M. Segoins and opened in August 1921. The four-story building contained dormitories for single young women who had moved to the city, a gymnasium, and a kindergarten. It provided meeting space for the local Boy Scouts and the Youth Division of the 1936 NAACP convention.

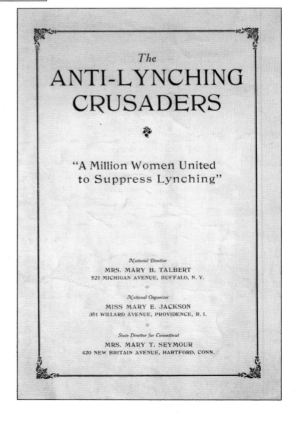

THE LILY-WHITE FRANCE COMBINE
"PICK AND SHOVEL" MARCHANT
"LILY-WHITE" CAMERON
"HUMANITARIAN" FRANCE

Senator France, who has asked the support of the colored voters because he is a "noble humanitarian" engineered the Philadelphia combine, including Roland Marchant and George W. Cameron. The open purpose of this combine is to control the Republican party in the State of Maryland. This means turning over to Roland Marchant, as Baltimore City boss, the interests of the thirty-six thousand colored Republicans of this city.

George W. Cameron is Roland Marchant's right hand man, and Roland Marchant and George W. Cameron have undertaken to deliver Baltimore City to Senator France. They have openly boasted that they control our vote. BY THEIR DEEDS YE SHALL KNOW THEM.

In giving out city positions, George W. Cameron, as City Chairman representing Roland Marchant, in the allotment of these jobs, wrote the letter we have had photographed and reproduced below, to the Republican Ward Executives of Baltimore:

THE REPUBLICAN CITY COMMITTEE FOR BALTIMORE CITY

GEORGE W. CAMERON, Chairman   EDWIN R. HARGETT, Jr., Secretary
R. FRANK SMITH, Vice-Chairman   WILLIAM G. ALBRECHT, Treasurer

March 16th 1922

My dear Friend:—

    Within the next ten days or two weeks, if you will submit me the names of ____ white men, who want labor-er's jobs at eighteen ($18.00) dollars per week for forty-eight hours, please let me have them at once.

    This is a pick and shovel job.

                                   Geo. W. Cameron

This letter shows that Messrs. Marchant and Cameron do not think that the colored Republican is even worthy of a "pick and shovel" job. If you are opposed to such race discrimination and injustice, then VOTE FOR JOHN W. GARRETT, the friend of Senator Weller and State Chairman Tait, who have got more jobs for colored Republicans in the past year than Senator France and all of his crowd in their whole lives. Colored voters, don't be fooled. A vote for "humanitarian" France is a vote for "pick and shovel" Marchant and "lily-white" Cameron.

COMMITTEE OF COLORED REPUBLICANS OF BALTIMORE.

COLORED REPUBLICANS OF THE COUNTY ATTENTION
If you oppose this race discrimination, even in pick and shovel jobs, join us colored Republicans of Baltimore, by voting against Senator France and his lily-white managers.

The Committee of Colored Republicans of Baltimore assisted Blacks in voting for candidates who worked to uplift the Black population. In this March 1922 letter, the committee criticized Republican senator Joseph France, George W. Cameron, and Roland Marchant of the Republican Committee of Baltimore City for their refusal to provide jobs to Blacks. The committee urged Blacks to vote for John W. Garrett, who would ensure that Black Baltimoreans received adequate employment.

The Anti-Lynching Crusaders was an interracial group of women dedicated to ending lynching in the United States. In this 1922 pamphlet, the organization detailed the number of lynchings of Black and white men, women, and children in each state. In August 1922, Mary E. Jackson, the group's national organizer, held weekly meetings at the Sharp Street Community House and encouraged the Baltimore chapter to assist the organization in its efforts to end lynching.

The
ANTI-LYNCHING
CRUSADERS

"A Million Women United
to Suppress Lynching"

National Director
MRS. MARY B. TALBERT
521 MICHIGAN AVENUE, BUFFALO, N. Y.

National Organizer
MISS MARY E. JACKSON
351 WILLARD AVENUE, PROVIDENCE, R. I.

State Director for Connecticut
MRS. MARY T. SEYMOUR
420 NEW BRITAIN AVENUE, HARTFORD, CONN.

The Baltimore Black Sox was a Negro League baseball team from 1913 until 1936. Three members of the 1922 team are pictured from left to right: captain Louis "Red" Miller, shortstop Spottswood Poles, and pitcher Anthony "Mac" Mahoney. During the 1920s, the Black Sox hosted a series of games against white major and minor league teams long before Major League Baseball was integrated. At one point, there were issues about Black umpires officiating the games.

The Delta Lambda Chapter of Alpha Phi Alpha Fraternity, Inc., established in Baltimore in 1919, has a long history of uplifting the Black community. In 1923, the fraternity hosted its annual "Go To School and Go To College" event, holding large meetings at schools, churches, and even parents' homes to encourage students to complete high school and go to college so they could advance civil rights.

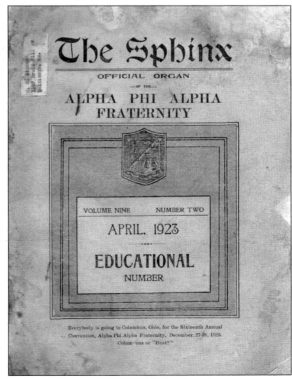

Dr. Edward Mayfield Boyle advocated against health disparities in the Black community. He publicly criticized white doctors who believed that Blacks were more susceptible to diseases such as tuberculosis. He believed this made white doctors less likely to treat Black patients because they thought there was little chance of curing them. He was a member of the Baltimore NAACP and recruited new members during their annual membership drives.

Florence Mills was a singer, dancer, and comedian who became an international star in *Lew Leslie's blackbirds*. In September 1924, Mills appeared at Baltimore's Academy Theatre in a production of *Dixie to Broadway* with an all-Black cast that included Shelton Brooks, Cora Green, and Will Vodery. Mills believed the production would give the Black actors an opportunity to showcase their talents and prove they were equal to white performers.

In November 1916, members of the Monumental Tennis Club, Baltimore's Black tennis organization, gathered with tennis professionals from nearby states and formed the American Tennis Association. The first national championship of the American Tennis Association was held at Druid Hill Park in 1917; it was held again in 1924, as shown on this program. The organization offered Black Baltimoreans the opportunity to compete against other Black tennis clubs without discrimination. A number of prominent individuals belonged to the club, including Dr. Harry S. McCard; longtime educator Ralph V. Cook; attorney Clarke L. Smith, who served on the Baltimore NAACP's executive committee; attorney and Elks leader Roy S. Bond; and suffragist Estelle Hall Young. The organization was eventually renamed the Baltimore Tennis Club.

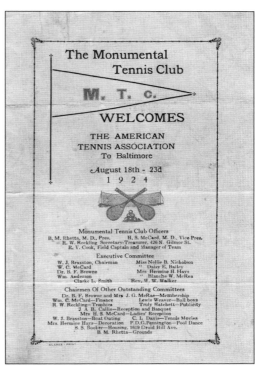

This vernacular image captured at Druid Hill Park shows the standard attire that women wore to play tennis during this time.

DEPARTMENT OF EDUCATION
STATE OF MARYLAND

No. 5598   Class

Elementary School Teacher's Certificate of the First Grade
Valid to teach in Colored Schools

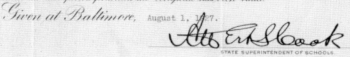

This is to certify that PATTIE ESTELLA HOLLOWAY *has satisfied the requirements of law necessary to make* her *eligible for appointment, in the State of Maryland, to the position of*

Assistant-Teacher in an Elementary School or Principal of a School
OF ONE OR TWO TEACHERS.

This certificate is valid for three years from date and renewable for four-year periods on evidence of successful experience and professional spirit and summer school credits earned within the last period for which the certificate has been valid.

Given at Baltimore, August 1, 1927.

STATE SUPERINTENDENT OF SCHOOLS.

In June 1925, the Defense League, headed by Black attorneys William Ashbie Hawkins and Warner T. McGuinn, sued Baltimore City over its unequal salary policy for teachers. Black teachers were paid half of what their white counterparts received. Hawkins and McGuinn argued that white teachers were paid higher salaries than Black teachers, and this violated the state's anti-discrimination law. The judge ruled in favor of the Defense League, but this decision was overturned by a higher court. This prompted Mayor Howard Jackson, in October 1926, to promise that teachers' salaries would be equal in the upcoming 1927 school year, and this was echoed by superintendent Dr. David Weglein. This allowed teachers like Pattie E. Holloway, pictured here, to receive salaries equal to those of white teachers.

Countee Cullen was a poet, novelist, playwright and the first husband of Nina Yolande Du Bois, daughter of sociologist, historian, and author W.E.B. Du Bois. In May 1926, Cullen was invited by the City Club to deliver a lecture at the Emerson Hotel. When the management saw that Cullen was Black, they informed the City Club that he could not speak at the hotel because their policy barred Blacks from going beyond the first floor.

The 1925 Frederick Douglass High School basketball team was part of the group of students that moved into a new building on Carey, Calhoun, and Baker Streets. The new high school was dedicated as Frederick Douglass High School in honor of the formerly enslaved abolitionist, orator, author, and native Marylander. This was the first public high school specifically built for Black students and had a gymnasium, library, and cafeteria.

Lillie Carroll Jackson's career in civil rights began when her daughters Juanita (left) and Virginia were denied admission to Maryland universities. Juanita was denied admission to the University of Maryland, and her sister Virginia was denied admission to the Maryland Institute College of Art. Jackson had a varied career that led her to civil rights. She worked as a washerwoman and teacher in Baltimore's colored school system. She was also an early Black female rental property owner, like her mother Amanda Bowen Carroll. In June 1928, Juanita, a Morgan College student, won the Baldwin Prize (pictured) for her oratorical skills. Her legendary skills were honed as a teenager at Frederick Douglass High School when she won the Toussaint Louverture Excellence in Declamation Award.

Ideal Building and Loan Association was established in the early 1920s by Teackle Wallis Lansey to assist Black families in securing mortgages to purchase homes and start businesses. In addition to daytime hours, the bank was also open on Thursday nights, the one night of the week that the staff of white households like cooks, maids, and butlers were off. At one point, it was the longest continuously Black-family-owned bank in Maryland.

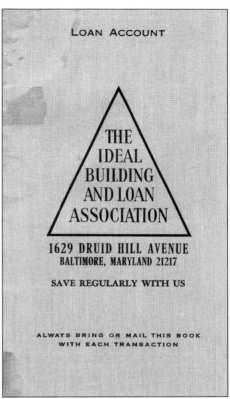

Fearless Williams (seated in front) was the maternal uncle to Thurgood Marshall, the nation's first Black Supreme Court justice. By 1926, Williams had one of the highest ranking jobs at the Baltimore & Ohio Railroad as a personal assistant to the company's president. He leveraged this position to obtain jobs for his relatives and friends and arranged for the railroad's linen to be washed at his brother-in-law's laundry, Druid Laundry, located at 1634 Druid Hill Avenue.

The Moorish Science Temple of America No. 13 was established in Baltimore at 705 South Sharp Street and was one of 15 temples across the country. The organization, founded in 1913 in Newark, New Jersey, by Prophet Noble Drew Ali, was modeled after Marcus Garvey's ideology of unity amongst all Africans. Followers were encouraged to become better citizens and to reject hate and embrace love.

This December 1928 ballot for Monumental Lodge No. 3 features several civil rights activists, one of which is attorney Josiah F. Henry Jr., the Baltimore NAACP's attorney and president of the Monumental Bar Association. In September 1928, Henry and his mother, Mary, purchased clothing from Stewart and Company, a white department store in downtown Baltimore. However, they could not try on the clothing due to the store's Jim Crow policy. Henry sent a letter to the store's manager and condemned their policy.

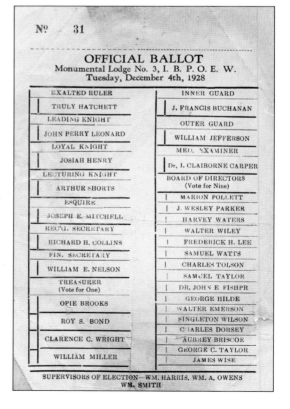

Three

THE GREAT DEPRESSION
1929–1940

As the nation grappled with the Great Depression, Baltimore's Black community found ways to survive and thrive. The Black population was about 142,000—up from 108,000 in 1920. The local NAACP had languished in the latter part of the 1920s, and membership had decreased. With encouragement from Carl J. Murphy, the *Afro-American Newspaper* editor and publisher, Lillie Carroll Jackson became the president of the NAACP and reshaped the organization into one dedicated to fighting segregation in all areas: education, employment, transportation, and housing. This culminated in 1938 with the nation's first lawsuit that attacked residential segregation ordinances and laid the foundation for *Shelley v. Kraemer* a decade later. Educational opportunities were expanded, and future city councilman Walter Thomas Dixon Sr. cofounded the Baltimore branch of the Cortez W. Peters Business School and trained Blacks for clerical and professional work through courses in shorthand, typing, accounting, and journalism. Coppin Normal School, the city's premier teacher-training institute, expanded from a two-year curriculum to three years due to an increased demand for qualified Black educators.

The decade also gave rise to a new generation of civil rights activists who sought to recruit more Black youth into the NAACP, Urban League, and other organizations. One fight that continued well into the 1930s—and for many decades—was over the absence of an anti-lynching bill. The 1931 lynching of Matthew Williams and the 1933 lynching of George Armwood, both on the Eastern Shore, garnered international attention and renewed calls for anti-lynching legislation, but to no avail. As the decade came to a close, Black Baltimoreans suffered a political loss when Warner T. McGuinn and William L. Fitzgerald completed their terms in 1931. It would be more than two decades before another Black person would break the color line at city hall. As 1940 approached, the country's entry into World War II loomed over all Baltimoreans—regardless of the color of their skin.

During the 1930s, Prophet Kiowa Costonie was known as one of the most active voices against racial inequality. In 1933, he spearheaded the Buy Where You Can Work campaign, which encouraged Blacks to boycott Pennsylvania Avenue businesses that refused to hire them. He contracted Thurgood Marshall as his attorney to handle negotiations with local merchants and the police. Marshall threatened to sue a merchant for $50,000 for defaming Costonie.

The Baltimore Symphony Orchestra performed a concert for Black adults in April 1930 at Frederick Douglass High School. Since the symphony performances were not integrated, the orchestra went into the Black community and performed at the high school. This helped to improve the musical appreciation and talents of the Black community by introducing them to well-trained musicians.

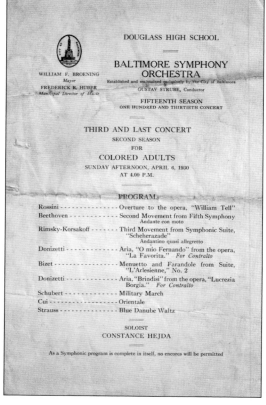

DOUGLASS HIGH SCHOOL

BALTIMORE SYMPHONY ORCHESTRA

Established and maintained exclusively by the City of Baltimore

WILLIAM F. BROENING
Mayor
FREDERICK R. HUBER
Municipal Director of Music

GUSTAV STRUBE, Conductor

FIFTEENTH SEASON
ONE HUNDRED AND THIRTIETH CONCERT

THIRD AND LAST CONCERT
SECOND SEASON
FOR
COLORED ADULTS
SUNDAY AFTERNOON, APRIL 6, 1930
AT 4.00 P.M.

PROGRAM

Rossini — Overture to the opera, "William Tell"
Beethoven — Second Movement from Fifth Symphony
Andante con moto
Rimsky-Korsakoff — Third Movement from Symphonic Suite, "Scheherazade"
Andantino quasi allegretto
Donizetti — Aria, "O mio Fernando" from the opera, "La Favorita." *For Contralto*
Bizet — Menuetto and Farandole from Suite, "L'Arlesienne," No. 2
Donizetti — Aria, "Brindisi" from the opera, "Lucrezia Borgia." *For Contralto*
Schubert — Military March
Cui — Orientale
Strauss — Blue Danube Waltz

SOLOIST
CONSTANCE HEJDA

As a Symphonic program is complete in itself, no encores will be permitted

46

Juanita Jackson's civil rights activism was inspired by her mother, Lillie Carroll Jackson, who led the Baltimore NAACP for over 30 years. In 1931, Juanita created the City-Wide Young People's Forum, a group of high school and college students galvanized for political activism. In 1936, Juanita established the NAACP Youth Boosters—with encouragement from Walter White—to increase membership. Her 1938 marriage to Clarence M. Mitchell Jr. united two families deeply involved in civil rights action.

Phone: Laf. 1208

Mrs. Lillie M. Jackson
President Baltimore Branch
N. A. A. C. P.

1216 Druid Hill Ave.   Baltimore, Md.

In 1933, Lillie Carroll Jackson was persuaded by Carl Murphy, editor and publisher of the *Afro-American Newspaper*, to serve as chairperson of the Baltimore NAACP's reorganization committee. In 1935, she was elected president and served until 1970. Under her leadership, the membership of the Baltimore branch rose from less than 200 in 1935 to over 25,000 in 1946. The address on her business card—1216 Druid Hill Avenue—was one of her homes.

THE MONUMENTAL CITY
BAR ASSOCIATION
14 E. PLEASANT STREET
BALTIMORE, MARYLAND

July 27, 1934.

Mr. Burdette B. Webster,
President, Baltimore City Bar Asso.,
309 Title Building,
Baltimore, Md.

Dear Sir:-

On August 23rd, 24th and 25th the
National Bar Association, composed of the leading Negro lawyers of the country, is holding its
annual convention here in Baltimore. The committee in charge of arrangements requests that
you address the assemblage on Thursday evening
August 23rd at the Sharp Street Memorial M. E.
Church, Dolphin and Etting Streets, at eight o'clock.

You will kindly let us have your acceptance
as soon as possible as the programmes must go to the
printers at an early date.

Yours very truly,

U. Grant Tyler
President

UGT/AEB

Harold Arthur Seaborne (right), educator and principal, tested the University of Maryland Law School's racial ban in January 1933 when he applied to the institution with support from the Baltimore NAACP. Although the university turned down Seaborne's application, a number of Black applicants, backed by the NAACP, challenged the law school's policy until the Maryland Court of Appeals ordered the admission of Donald Gaines Murray in 1935.

The Monumental City Bar Association was founded by Black lawyers who were denied entry to the white Bar Association of Baltimore City. The organization held monthly meetings where they discussed Jim Crow laws and how to fight them in court. Several civil rights activists served as presidents, including Ulysses Grant Tyler, who signed this 1934 letter. In 1933, Tyler and a group of lawyers met with Gov. Albert Ritchie and demanded that he pass an anti-lynching bill.

In October 1936, the Colored Republicans Voters' League of Maryland held a Young Republicans' Rally at the Fifth Regiment Armory, which is listed on the National Register of Historic Places. Many notable Blacks gave speeches, including Willard W. Allen, Grand Worshipful Master of the Masons; and Jesse Owens, winner of four gold medals at the 1936 Olympic Games. Others on the program included Maryland governor Harry W. Nice and real estate broker Marse Callaway.

During the 1930s, Black high school and college students formed their own social, literary, cultural, and civic organizations where they could fellowship and uplift one another. Lucille Watts and some friends formed the Tahigwa Sub Debs, a group that held dances, teas, birthday parties, and other celebrations at buildings owned by Black organizations, including the Odd Fellows Hall, Pythian Castle, and the York Hotel. They hired Black musicians, including Bubby Johnson's Plantation Orchestra and Rivers Chambers.

Young Republicans' Rally

Auspices of

The Colored Republican Voters' League of Maryland

At Fifth Regiment Armory
October 2nd, 1936, at 9:00 p. m.

PROGRAMME:

The meeting called to order by Marse S. Callaway, President of the Colored Republican Voters' League of Maryland

SONG—"America .... Audience
INVOCATION ....Rev. C. C. Ferguson, D. D.
INTRODUCTORY REMARKS.................Robert P. McGuinn
  Chairman of the Young Republicans of Maryland and Master of Ceremonies
ADDRESS OF WELCOME..........The Honorable Harry W. Nice, *Governor of Maryland*
ADDRESS ....Francis E. Rivers,
  Director of The Eastern Division of Colored Republicans
MUSIC................................The Morgan College Singers
ADDRESS...............Former Senator Joseph Irvin France
ADDRESS.........................Hon. Harry O. Levin,
  Maryland Director of Landon-Knox Clubs
ADDRESS ....Raymond Pace Alexander,
  President of Philadelphia Bar Association
REMARKS ....William P. Lawson,
  Chairman Republican State Central Committee of Maryland
ADDRESS ....Frederick Morrow,
  Director of Young Colored Republicans of the East
ADDRESS ....Rev. W. E. King of New York
ADDRESS ....Willard W. Allen,
  Grand Master of Masons
MUSIC ....
ADDRESS .... Jesse Owens,
  International Champion of Sprinters and idol of young People everywhere
INTRODUCTION OF VISITORS...............Marse S. Callaway

OFFICERS

Bernice Morris - - President
Juanita Mayden - Vice President
Beatrice Scott - - Secretary
Margaret Smith - Fin. Secretary
Florine Jones - - Treasurer
Virginia Thomas - Business Manager

MEMBERS

Lottie Bazzle   Elvira Butler
Cecelia Franklin   Alice Willis
Reginia Bartlett   Sara Duvall

Tahigwa Sub-Debs

requests the honor of presence at their

Post-Easter Dance

at the

New Albert Hall

Thursday, April 16, 1936

from 9:30 until?

Lyrics by Bubby Johnson

25 cents before 9:30 - 35 cents after

SWANKS CLUB Will be HONORED GUEST

Rev. Edmond D. Meade was the longtime pastor of Israel Baptist Church in historic East Baltimore. Meade dedicated 50 years to the Baltimore Branch of the NAACP, for which he served on the executive board and led membership drives. He was nicknamed "Mr. Civil Rights" because of his dedication to the cause. In 1937, the nation's first suit opposing restrictive housing covenants in homeowner's deeds was filed by the Baltimore NAACP on behalf of Reverend Meade. In 1936, he attempted to purchase property at 2227 Barclay Street in an all-white block. A lawsuit was filed against him by white neighbors through attorney William L. Marbury Jr. The NAACP saw this as a test case to overturn residential segregation laws in Baltimore, but unfortunately, they lost the case.

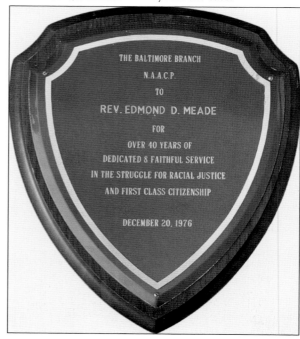

THE BALTIMORE BRANCH
N.A.A.C.P.
TO
REV. EDMOND D. MEADE
FOR
OVER 40 YEARS OF
DEDICATED & FAITHFUL SERVICE
IN THE STRUGGLE FOR RACIAL JUSTICE
AND FIRST CLASS CITIZENSHIP

DECEMBER 20, 1976

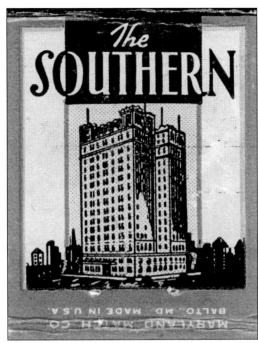

The Southern Hotel had a long history of segregation—it banned Blacks from entering unless they were attending a predominantly white gathering. In some cases, Blacks had to use the freight elevator while whites used the regular elevator. This applied to Bubby Johnson's Plantation Orchestra, who performed there in November 1936 at a dance. The hotel's Jim Crow policy was similar to those of other lodgings in downtown Baltimore, such as the Emerson and Lord Baltimore Hotels. In 1960, the Southern became the last major hotel to drop its discriminatory practice.

Musicians Protective Association

LOCAL UNION NO. 543 A. F. OF M, BALTIMORE, MD.

Contract Blank for Bubby Johnson's
Plantation Orchestra

Baltimore, Md. Nov. 30th 1936

The undersigned, as party of the first part and second part respectively as follows:

The party of the first part agrees to furnish 13 Musicians, members of Local Union No. 543 American Federation of Musicians, AS THEIR AGENT, to the party of the second part, for the sum of $.85.00 beng wages for

Dance engagement Southern Hotel Balto.Md.
On the said night of Saturday Jan.9th,1937
Time from 10:PM—2:AM Recd.$15.00 forfeit
Balance Due $.70.00. to be paid at Intermission in small bills

Bubby Johnson
Party of the First Part
S.O. Golbug
Party of the Second Part

The above contract to be subject to the rules of Local Union No. 543 of the American Federation of Musicians.

"All contracts must be filed with the Secretary within one week after the sign. of thereof, and no contract is valid until accepted by the Executive Committee."
As the musicians engaged under the stipulations of this contract are members of the American Federation of Musicians nothing in this shall ever be so construced as to interfere with any obligation which the musicans owe to the A.F. of M by reason of thier prior obligation to the A.F. of M. as members thereof

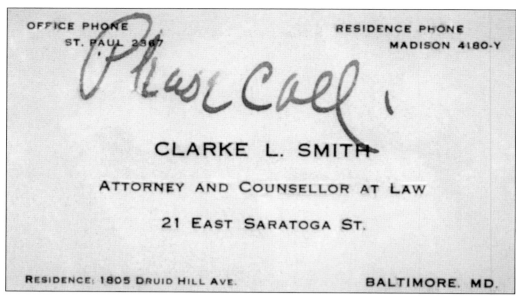

Attorney Clarke L. Smith broke residential segregation laws in August 1935 when he purchased a home in an all-white block of West Franklin Street. The practice was known as blockbusting, where Blacks moved into white neighborhoods, forcing them to integrate or sell to Black homeowners. Twenty years earlier, Smith had purchased a home on McCulloh Street, which prompted threats from white neighbors. Eventually, white residents moved out, and by 1935, McCulloh Street was predominantly Black.

All Bills must be Paid before Any Interment can be made in this Lot.

PHONE, LAFAYETTE 1193

BALTIMORE, June 23 1937

Mrs. Ella Milbourne

1327 Myrtle Ave

To THE TRUSTEES of MT. AUBURN CEMETERY, Drs.,

OFFICE : 1206 - 1210 ETTING STREET

1937

To Care of Lot No. 166 in Area Mt. Brown For 15 Years ending 1937 $15.00

RECEIVED PAYMENT

Trustees of Mt. Auburn Cemetery

Per Emma Smith

Mount Auburn Cemetery, established in 1872, was the largest burial ground for Blacks and was owned by Sharp Street Memorial Episcopal Church. Since Blacks could not be interred in white cemeteries, and Laurel, the other major Black cemetery, was in decline, Mount Auburn offered families a chance to bury their dead with dignity in a place where plots were maintained for a fee. In 1937, Ella Milbourne paid $15 for perpetual care of a relative's plot.

Herbert Milton Frisby was a science teacher at Frederick Douglass High School and principal of Douglass's Evening School. The evening school provided adults with an opportunity to get a high school diploma in vocational trades such as dressmaking, journalism, and nursing. At the 1930 commencement, Martin M. Hihn, the white director of evening schools, pointed out that 12 percent of Black people were illiterate. Hihn said he hoped the graduates would help to reduce the illiteracy rate.

Florence Snowden (second from right) was the younger sister of Lillie Carroll Jackson. In 1941, Snowden was honored by the *Afro-American Newspaper* for her efforts to protect Black homeowners from commercial development. In 1936, she formed the Northwest Residential Protective Association to guard Black homeowners in Northwest Baltimore against companies that wanted to erect businesses in their neighborhoods.

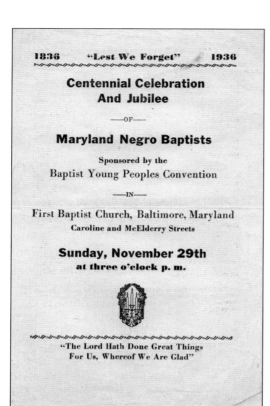

1836   "Lest We Forget"   1936

Centennial Celebration And Jubilee

—OF—

Maryland Negro Baptists

Sponsored by the
Baptist Young Peoples Convention

—IN—

First Baptist Church, Baltimore, Maryland
Caroline and McElderry Streets

Sunday, November 29th
at three o'clock p. m.

"The Lord Hath Done Great Things
For Us, Whereof We Are Glad"

In 1936, Black Maryland Baptists celebrated the centennial of their formation. This program paid homage to William Crane and Moses Clayton, who established the first Baptist Sunday school and organized First Baptist Church, the city's oldest Baptist church, with 10 members. The organization also paid tribute to the white and Black men and women "who bore the burden and heat of the day" and provided a way for the Black Baptist movement to grow.

The Faculty Of

Dunbar High School

Presents The

9A Classes

In

Closing Exercises

IN THE SCHOOL AUDITORIUM

MONDAY MORNING
JUNE 23th, 1941
10:30 A. M.

In 1940, Dunbar High School awarded its first diplomas to the senior class. Prior to this, the school only served students until the 11th grade; they then had to go to Frederick Douglass High School in West Baltimore for 12th grade. The school fulfilled a need for students as well as the East Baltimore community, as professional concerts, plays, and state educational meetings were held there.

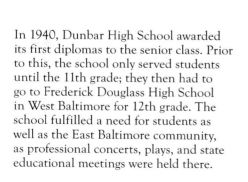

Crowded conditions and a lack of indoor plumbing and sanitation caused diseases to be rampant in Baltimore. The Black community suffered immensely due to lack of funding and available clinics. In 1930, the Baltimore City Health Department established immunization clinics for children to control diphtheria. This list shows that there were more white clinics than Black clinics. Nonetheless, Black parents could get their children immunized at Metropolitan United Methodist Church and four schools, including Frederick Douglass High School.

VACCINATION AND IMMUNIZATION CLINICS.

FOR WHITE CHILDREN ONLY.

Odd Fellow's Hall, Hillsdale, Forest Park Ave. nr. Weathersville Rd.,Fri.at 9.30 A.M.
School 60, Francis St. & Clifton Ave., Tues. & Thurs. at 11.30 A. M.
School 65, Poplar Grove & Lanvale Sts., Fridays at 2 P. M.
School 93, Central Ave. & Lexington St., Mon. Wed. & Thurs. at 1 P. M.
School 76, Fort Ave. & Decatur St., Thursdays at 2 P. M.
Chester & Preston Sts., Mondays at 1 P. M.
1736 E. North Ave., Wednesdays at 12.30 P. M.
School 6, Fleet & Ann Sts., Fridays at 2 P. M.
4000 Pennington Ave., Fridays at 1 P. M.
School 64, Maine & Garrison Aves., Thursdays at 10 A. M.
2216 Frederick Ave., Mondays at 1 P. M.
School 13, Patterson Park Ave. & McElderry St., Wednesdays at 1.30 P. M.
918 Russell St., Fridays at 1 P. M.
Faith Chapel, Broadway & Gay Sts., Fridays at 1 P. M.
414 S. Highland Ave., Thursdays at 10 A. M.
1418 Light St., Tuesdays at 12.30 P. M.
6th & Patapsco Sts., Thursdays at 1 P. M.
School 223, Oakley Ave. & Pimlico Rd., Tuesdays at 12.30 P. M.

FOR WHITE AND COLORED CHILDREN.

Robert Garrett Hosp., 27 N. Carey St., daily except Saturdays at 9 A. M.
Balto. City Health Dept..8th floor, Municipal Bldg., Mon. & Thurs. at 2.30 P. M.
1914 McElderry St., Tues. & Thurs. at 2 P. M., Sat. at 10 A. M.
914 E. Madison St., Tues. & Fri. at 1 P. M.
447 E. 25th St., Tues. at 2 P. M.
Valley & Biddle St., Fridays at 1 P. M.

FOR COLORED CHILDREN ONLY.

Douglass High School, Baker & Calhoun Sts., Tues. at 9.30 A. M.
School 122, Preston St. & Druid Hill Ave., Mondays at 9 A. M.
Metropolitan Church, Lanvale & Carrollton Ave., Mon. at 11.30 A. M.
(Carrollton Ave. entrance)
School 154, Fairfield, Wednesdays at 1 P. M.
School 106, Hill St. nr. Sharp, Mon. Wed. Fri. at 9 A. M.

7.1.30

The Delta Lambda Chapter of Alpha Phi Alpha Fraternity, Inc., was established in May 1919. Several of its presidents became leading civil rights activists, including Furman L. Templeton (back row, second from right), William Alfred Carroll Hughes Jr. (back row, on Templeton's left), and Miles Washington Connor (front row, third from left). Hughes served as the legal counsel for the Baltimore NAACP for 30 years. In 1939, he won the case to equalize Black and white teachers' salaries throughout Maryland.

Peabody Conservatory of Music refused admission to Blacks until 1949, when Paul Archibald Brent was accepted as the first Black student. Brent, who graduated in 1953, grew up surrounded by music; his father, Howard, directed the choir at Allen AME Church, and his mother, Lavinia, was a pianist. Brent learned to play the piano at age five, and when he graduated from Frederick Douglass High School in 1946, he wrote the class song. After serving in the military, Brent returned to Baltimore and applied to Peabody. The school's director, Reginald Stewart, had long wanted to abolish the ban on Blacks, so he used Brent's application as a test case.

Four

FROM JIM CROW TO BROWN v. BOARD OF EDUCATION
1941–1954

When the United States entered World War II in December 1941, the impact was felt from the schools to the workplace. Frederick Douglass High School, Dunbar High School, Carver Vocational Technical High School, Coppin Teachers College, and Morgan State College saw a reduced number of male students during the war. Businesses, churches, and community organizations also felt the impact.

This caused many to ask the same questions raised during World War I: How could Blacks fight for freedom abroad, yet be denied basic rights at home? How could the United States promote unity and patriotism when its army was segregated? Bayard Rustin, a prominent civil rights activist, summed it up when he stated, "While there is a very real question whether any army can bring freedom, certainly a Jim Crow army cannot." Nonetheless, thousands of Black men and women enlisted to serve with the belief that their patriotism would lead to equal rights in the United States.

On the home front, Saul Perdue, Furman L. Templeton, the Baltimore NAACP, the Baltimore Urban League, and the Congress of Industrial Organizations forced the Glenn L. Martin Company, one of the largest wartime defense contractors, to hire skilled Black workers, including hundreds of Black women.

As older civil rights activists retired or died, a new generation formed with the goal of ending legalized segregation across the city. The NAACP launched several lawsuits against discriminatory practices in public venues, including golf courses and the Enoch Pratt Free Library, abolishing some of the last vestiges of Jim Crow. Other institutions, like the fire and police departments, employed Blacks, ending a decades-long ban.

Almost 20 years after Donald Gaines Murray integrated the University of Maryland Law School, three Black women obtained their law degrees from the university: Juanita Jackson Mitchell and Elaine Davis in 1950 and Lena King Lee in 1952. Their integration of and graduation from the school marked a new era in Black women's involvement in civil rights and laid the foundation for them to break another barrier in the realm of politics.

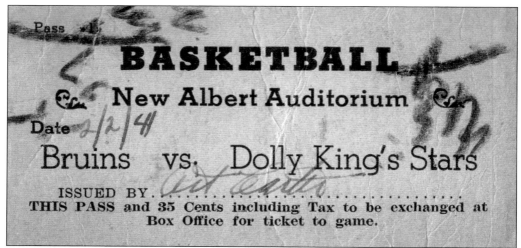

Pass

BASKETBALL
New Albert Auditorium

Date 2/2/41

Bruins vs. Dolly King's Stars

ISSUED BY Art Carter

THIS PASS and 35 Cents including Tax to be exchanged at Box Office for ticket to game.

Arthur M. Carter was a sports reporter and managing editor of the *Afro-American* newspapers. Carter was one of the few Black correspondents in World War II and covered North Africa and Italy, along with fellow *Afro* reporter Ollie Stewart. In 1941, he attended a basketball game between Dolly King's Stars and the Bruins at the New Albert Auditorium on Pennsylvania Avenue.

Arthur "Smokestack" Hardy was the first Black auxiliary firefighter certified in Baltimore in 1942. The start of World War II caused a shortage of firefighters. As a result, the Baltimore Fire Department was forced to integrate. Hardy, an avid collector of Black firefighter memorabilia, wrote letters to people across the country to inquire about historic Black firefighters. In 1949, he formed the SHC Fire Buff Club and advocated for paid auxiliary service. The Arthur Smoke Stack Hardy Fire Station on McMechen Street is named for him.

Dr. Ralph Jonathan Young (first row, fourth from right) was a prominent East Baltimorean who served the community for over 40 years. On April 24, 1942, Dr. Young was part of the March on Annapolis, a gathering of prominent Black citizens in Maryland's capital to demand civil rights from the government. Young asked for Black participation on the Maryland Tuberculosis Commission, urging the governor to allow Black Baltimoreans to "have a part in the administration of black medical institutions." In 1944, Dr. Young was appointed the first Black clinician at Johns Hopkins Hospital, and in 1946, he became the first Black staff member at the hospital. He was also a member of the Iota Chapter of Chi Delta Mu, the Black medical fraternity. The program at right incorrectly lists Dr. Young's middle name as "James" instead of Jonathan.

TESTIMONIAL DINNER

honoring

Doctor Ralph James Young

SUNDAY, OCTOBER SECOND
nineteen hundred and sixty-six
FOUR O'CLOCK P. M.

SHERATON-BELVEDERE HOTEL
BALTIMORE, MARYLAND

COMMUNITY ~~NTERS~~

The recreation buildings are ope. daily to serve the social ~~a~~d cultural needs of the whole co. munity; to provide a meeting place for small club groups a..d large neighborhood assemblies and, as far as facilities permit, to foster the recreational interests of all ages.

The activities for children include game., stories, contests, music, folk dances, clubs, hand-work, block b..ilding.

The activities for youth and adults inclu..e clubs, social dances, parties, hobbies, crafts, music, drama, badminton, table games, table tennis, deck tennis, athletics.

CHICK WEBB MEMORIAL RECREATION CENTER
    632 N. Eden Street
        Monday through Friday, 2-10 P. M.; Saturday, 1-7 P. M.
        L. C. Nixon, Executive Director

LEXINGTON STREET RECREATION CENTER
    732-34 W. Lexington Street
        Monday through Friday, 2-10 P. M.
        Christo L. Waller, Director

CHERRY HILL HOMES RECREATION CENTER
    2700 Spelman Road
        Monday & Thursday, 3-11 P. M.; Tuesday, 2-10 P. M.
    Wednesday & Friday, 10-6 P. M.
        Mrs. Alice Parham, Director

FREDERICK DOUGLASS HOMES RECREATION CENTER
    Lexington Street near Caroline Street
        Monday, Wednesday & Thursday, 2-10 P. M.
    Tuesday & Friday, 12-8 P. M.
        Miss Erma Holland, Director

McCULLOH HOMES RECREATION CENTER
    1010 McCulloh Street
        Monday through Thursday, 2-10 P. M.; Friday, 11-7 P. M.

HOUSING PROJECTS

GILMOR HOMES RECREATION CENTER
    1515 Vincent Court—Monday through Friday, 2-10 P. M.
        Mrs. Hattie B. Smith, Director

HOLABIRD HOMES RECREATION CENTER
    1700 Bobwhite Avenue—Monday through Friday, 3-6 P. M.
        Tuesday, Wednesday & Thursday, 7-10 P. M.

SOMERSET HOMES RECREATION CENTER
    500 N. Central Avenue—Monday through Friday, 2:30-5:30 P. M.

• 2 •

This is a list of the recreation centers and playgrounds available for Black children in 1949. At the top of the list is the Chick Webb Memorial Recreation Center. After drummer and bandleader Webb died in 1939, Dr. Ralph J. Young, Webb's physician, honored the musician by establishing the center in East Baltimore in 1947. The center fulfilled a need in the Black East Baltimore community, which lacked adequate recreational facilities in the schools.

John Earl Stokes III was a pioneering car salesman at Stu Berger Oldsmobile and later sold Oldsmobiles at the A.D. Anderson dealership. He was a successful salesman because he developed a clientele among Black educators, postal workers, and Bethlehem Steel employees. Stokes taught mechanical arts, mechanical drawing, and sheet metal work at Clifton Park Junior High School.

Charles Hamilton Houston was a prominent lawyer, former dean of Howard University Law School, and Thurgood Marshall's mentor and close friend. Houston was the lead attorney for Louise Kerr's lawsuit against the Enoch Pratt Free Library's restriction against Black women in their training classes. In his final case, he represented Esther E. McCready, who had been rejected from the University of Maryland Nursing School on the basis of race. McCready, a 1949 graduate of Dunbar High School, along with Houston and Thurgood Marshall, appealed the case to the Maryland Court of Appeals and won. Charles Hamilton Houston School 181, located on Baker and Calhoun Streets, was named in his honor.

Charles Hamilton Houston
Junior High School
DEPARTMENT OF EDUCATION, BALTIMORE, MARYLAND

By Authority of the Board of School Commissioners this

Certificate

has been awarded to

Reginald van Michael Stokely

in Testimony of the Satisfactory Completion of the Course of Study Prescribed for the Ninth Grade

Frank J Sorrell
PRINCIPAL

Walter Sondheim Jr.
PRESIDENT OF BOARD OF SCHOOL COMMISSIONERS

June 15, 1956

John N Fischer
SUPERINTENDENT OF PUBLIC INSTRUCTION

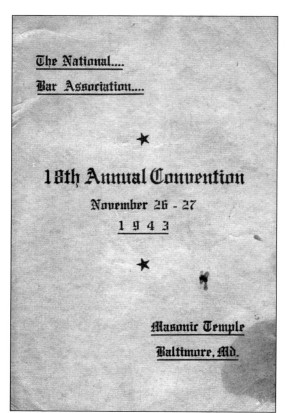

The National.... Bar Association....

★

18th Annual Convention

November 26 - 27

1943

★

Masonic Temple

Baltimore, Md.

The National Bar Association was founded in 1925 for Black lawyers who were excluded from the white American Bar Association. In 1943, the organization held its annual convention at the Masonic Temple in Baltimore. Speakers included Thurgood Marshall, special counsel for the NAACP, who discussed how Black lawyers were working to abolish discriminatory laws, and William H. Hastie Jr., the dean of Howard University Law School, who elaborated upon discrimination in the Armed Forces.

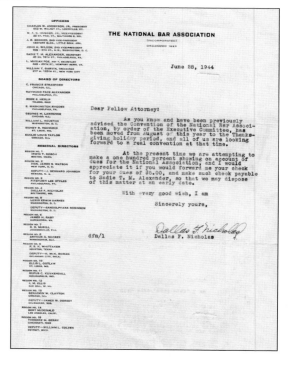

The 1944 letter pictured here discussed moving the National Bar Association convention from August to November and was signed by Dallas F. Nicholas Sr., regional director of the association. In 1948, Nicholas and his law partner William I. Gosnell received nationwide attention when they sued Baltimore City to lift racial bans on golf courses. Until then, only one course at Carroll Park was open to Black golfers, and it was much smaller than the ones available to white golfers. There is an elementary school named after Nicholas.

In 1943, Louise Kerr (middle) filed a federal lawsuit against the Enoch Pratt Free Library after she was denied admission to a library training course because she was Black. Carl J. Murphy, publisher of the *Afro-American*, and Lillie Carroll Jackson, president of the NAACP, encouraged Kerr to file the lawsuit. She and her father, Dr. Thomas Henderson Kerr, were represented by attorneys Charles Hamilton Houston (left) and William Alfred Carroll Hughes Jr. (right). Houston and Hughes argued that the library, as a public institution that received funds from the city, could not bar Blacks from the training course. In 1944, US District Court Judge Calvin W. Chestnut dismissed the suit, saying the library was a private corporation, not a governmental agency. Kerr's lawyers then appealed to the Fourth Circuit Court of Appeals in Richmond, Virginia, and in April 1945 the court ruled that since the library was an "instrumentality of the State of Maryland," they could not deny Kerr admission to the program. A week later, the Pratt Library Board of Trustees appealed to the US Supreme Court, but it declined to hear the case. The board subsequently rescinded its policy barring Black applicants from the training program, but Louise Kerr never reapplied for the program.

Virginia Jackson Kiah, educator and artist, was the daughter of Lillie Carroll Jackson, civil rights activist and longtime Baltimore NAACP president. Virginia worked alongside her mother and siblings at voter registration drives and protests and served as the membership secretary of the Baltimore NAACP. When Lillie died in 1975, she willed her home at 1320 Eutaw Place to Virginia, who turned it into a museum. The Lillie Carroll Jackson Civil Rights Museum is still in operation today.

In this February 1945 letter on Baltimore NAACP letterhead, Virginia Kiah is writing to her brother-in-law Brewington Kiah. Brewington had experienced discrimination at his World War II military base in Florida and was asking for assistance from the Baltimore NAACP. Virginia assured him that the letter was forwarded to the NAACP's Veterans Administration, and attorneys Leslie Perry and Thurgood Marshall were diligently working on his case.

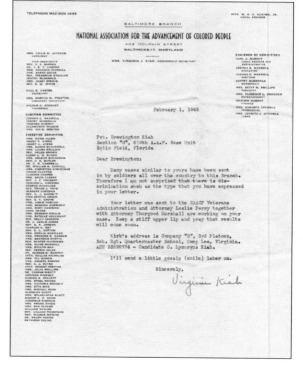

Mary Eliza Waters Risteau, a pioneering white female Harford County legislator, attended a reception at the governor's mansion in Annapolis in March 1951. When she saw Black guests, Risteau became disgusted and exited through a side door. When stopped by a guard who told her to use the front door, she replied, "Don't make me go back through that crowd." Her comments were reported in the *Baltimore Sun* in an article titled, "Negro Guests at Governor's Mansion, Exit Miss Risteau." In response, Rosina Cole penned a scathing letter in which she criticized Risteau's racism. Cole was the mother of educator and activist Pearl Cole and Judge Harry A. Cole, the first Black man elected to the Maryland State Senate. She reminded Risteau that the "colored people who attended Governor [Theodore] McKeldin's reception were some of our finest American citizens." Cole sent it to the *Baltimore Sun*, but they refused to print it.

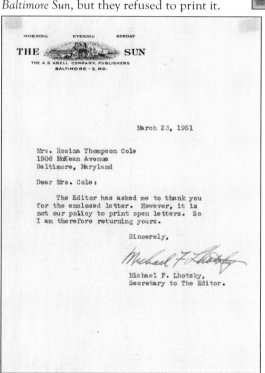

Mrs. Rosina Thompson Cole
1906 McKean Ave.
Baltimore 17, Md.

An open Letter to —

Miss Mary E. W. Risteau
Harford County Legislator
Annapolis. Md.

My dear Miss Risteau:
   You have my deepest sympathy. I am sincerely sorry for you and all people like you, who suffer from such ignorance. The Colored People who attended Governor McKeldins Reception were some of our finest American citizens and you probably missed

MORNING   EVENING   SUNDAY

THE   SUN

THE A. S. ABELL COMPANY, PUBLISHERS
BALTIMORE - 3, MD.

March 23, 1951

Mrs. Rosina Thompson Cole
1906 McKean Avenue
Baltimore, Maryland

Dear Mrs. Cole:

   The Editor has asked me to thank you for the enclosed letter. However, it is not our policy to print open letters. So I am therefore returning yours.

Sincerely,

Michael F. Lhotsky,
Secretary to The Editor.

FREDERICK ISADORE SCOTT

Vision
To attend U. S. M. M. C. C
To be an engineer

Frederick Isadore Scott Jr. was the grandson of Rev. Garnett Russell Waller Sr., pastor of Baltimore's Trinity Baptist Church. In 1950, Scott received his chemical engineering degree from Johns Hopkins University as the first Black undergraduate in its history. He described his experience at Hopkins as socially isolating and said his integration occurred "without much fuss." Scott's actions were influential; a group of Black Johns Hopkins alumni created the Fred Scott Brigade to pay homage to him. In 2022, Johns Hopkins University named a residential building in Scott's honor.

DICK CAMPBELL
PRESENTS
HAZEL SCOTT
Pianist

SPONSORED BY
KAPPA CHAPTER
IOTA PHI LAMBDA SORORITY

POLYTECHNIC AUDITORIUM
BALTIMORE, MARYLAND

SUNDAY, JANUARY 27, 1952
AT 5 O'CLOCK

PRESENTED FOR BENEFIT OF SCHOLARSHIP FUND

Hazel Scott was a pianist who was known for combining jazz sounds with classical music. In January 1952, she performed for the Kappa Chapter of Iota Phi Lambda, a Black sorority for professional women, at the Polytechnic High School Theatre before it was integrated later that year. In the 1950s, Scott became the first Black woman to have her own television show.

Anne Beadenkopf, a noted white portrait painter, was a life member of the NAACP. Beadenkopf felt that she could best dismantle discrimination through her paintings of prominent Blacks, including former NAACP executive director Walter White, Thurgood Marshall, and drummer and bandleader Chick Webb. Beadenkopf taught art classes at the Chick Webb Memorial Recreation Center. She used the proceeds from her commissions to combat Jim Crow transportation laws. She was a member of the Baltimore Urban League and close friends with Virginia Jackson Kiah, to whom this letter is addressed. In 1953, Beadenkopf was honored by the Zeta Phi Beta Sorority, Inc., a Black sorority, as "Woman of the Year" for her dedication to civil rights.

Dear Virginia:
Find enclosed the promised photograph of my painting "French Lady".
What did your family think about the other photographs?
Hope you had a delightful and restful visit at the seashore.
Give me a ring when you return to Baltimore next week-end, won't you?
Love,
Anne Beadenkopf

7-20-53

MARIAN ANDERSON   LYRIC THEATRE BALTIMORE, MD.

Marian Anderson was an American contralto who performed throughout the United States and Europe. In 1953, the Lyric Theatre in Baltimore refused to let Anderson perform there, which generated backlash from the white and Black communities. Many citizens complained to the Lyric's owners and threatened to boycott the theater. Finally, Maryland's Commission on Interracial Relations persuaded the Lyric's owners to let Anderson perform there on January 8, 1954.

Dr. H. Maceo Williams (left) is pictured at his daughter's wedding in 1949. Williams was the director of the segregated Druid Hill Health Center and the first Black to be hired by the Baltimore City Health Department. Williams was concerned with the high rates of tuberculosis in the Black community and wrote to Gov. Herbert O'Conor about finding a solution. In 1944, O'Conor appointed Williams as the first Black to serve on the Maryland Tuberculosis Sanatorium Commission.

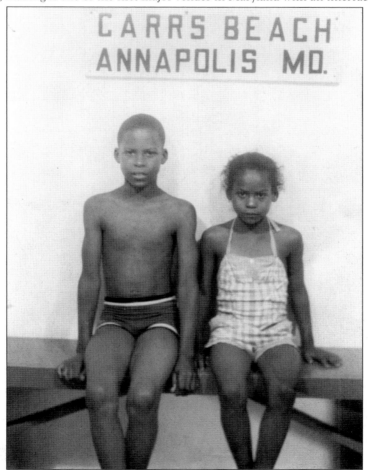

Carr's Beach was founded in 1926 by Frederick Carr and his wife, Mary Wells Carr, as a beach retreat for Black families in Annapolis. Their daughter, Elizabeth Carr Smith, operated Carr's Beach, and her sister, Florence Carr Sparrow, opened the adjoining Sparrow's Beach in 1931. When Elizabeth died in 1948, her son Frederick partnered with Baltimore businessman, numbers runner, and philanthropist William "Little Willie" Adams and created the Carr's Beach Amusement Company. Adams invested $150,000 in Carr's recreation and entertainment facilities. Carr's Beach was a safe haven for Blacks who came to enjoy music and the waterfront. The beach also attracted white visitors, making it one of the first major venues in Maryland with an interracial clientele.

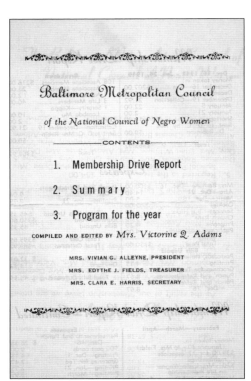

Baltimore Metropolitan Council

of the National Council of Negro Women

— CONTENTS —

1. Membership Drive Report

2. Summary

3. Program for the year

COMPILED AND EDITED BY *Mrs. Victorine Q. Adams*

MRS. VIVIAN G. ALLEYNE, PRESIDENT

MRS. EDYTHE J. FIELDS, TREASURER

MRS. CLARA E. HARRIS, SECRETARY

The Baltimore Metropolitan Council of the National Association of Negro Women was founded in 1943 by Juanita Jackson Mitchell, Victorine Quille Adams, Vivian Alleyene, Emma Dudley, and Kate Sheppherd to address the political needs of Black women. They encouraged women to become more politically active and laid the foundation for the first Black women in Maryland's government, such as Victorine Q. Adams, Verda F. Welcome, Lena King Lee, and Irma G. Dixon in the 1950s and 1960s. In 1945, they endorsed a state bill that repealed decades old Jim Crow transportation laws.

After World War II, many Black veterans used their GI benefits to enroll in vocational and technical training classes, such as the New York Tech Television class. This course, taught by William Edward Griggs (first row, fourth from right), a World War II veteran, instructed men how to repair televisions—an invaluable skill at the time. Vocational courses offered an opportunity for Black veterans who wanted to learn a trade and become economically stable for themselves and their families.

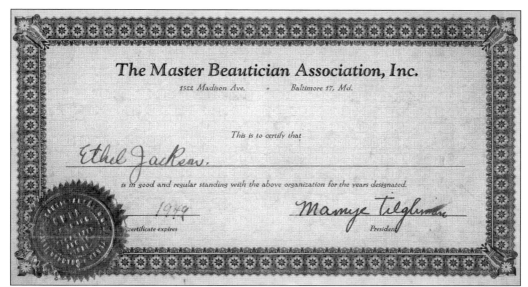

The Master Beautician Association, Inc.

1522 Madison Ave.   •   Baltimore 17, Md.

This is to certify that

Ethel Jackson.

is in good and regular standing with the above organization for the years designated.

1949

certificate expires

Mamie Tilghman

President

In 1941, attorney W.A.C. Hughes Jr. threatened to sue the state over a beautician's amendment that he believed placed a financial burden on Black beauticians due to increased license fees that would result in massive unemployment. Virgie Waters, president of the Colored Master Beauticians' Association of Maryland, said that beautician shops were never properly inspected by the white inspectors and called for more Blacks to be appointed as inspectors.

Baltimore native Thurgood Marshall was honored in 1953 at Morgan State College for his numerous civil rights accomplishments. In his 20-year legal career, he had successfully defended Black soldiers who were unfairly court-martialed during World War II, argued for Black voters' rights in Texas primary elections, and got restrictive housing covenants overturned. At that time, Marshall had won 12 victories before the Supreme Court and assisted in 15 other cases.

A TESTIMONIAL DINNER

IN HONOR OF

Mr. Human Rights
"MR. CIVIL RIGHTS"

THURGOOD MARSHALL

sponsored by

Monumental City Bar Associaton

Sunday evening, February 15th, 1953

SIX O'CLOCK

MORGAN COLLEGE REFECTORY

Baltimore, Maryland

Walter Green Post No. 14 is the oldest and largest Black American Legion post in Maryland. The group's headquarters were at 1308 McCulloh Street, and they assisted World War II veterans with claiming GI benefits and processed claims for widows. The post secured jobs for veterans during the Depression and pushed for the passage of an anti-lynching bill. This 1947 membership application was for John H. Davis of 1048 West Lexington Street.

The Baltimore Police Department had a ban against Blacks joining the police force until 1938, when four Black men were hired—but not allowed to wear uniforms. In 1943, Black police officers were allowed to wear uniforms, and in 1947, James Hiram Butler Jr. became the first Black officer promoted to sergeant. By 1950, there were 50 Black officers in the department.

Ethel Lavinia Weems Jackson, pictured with her husband, was one of the first 12 women hired as mail carriers in 1943. The women were temporarily hired by the Baltimore Post Office to relieve the shortage of postal workers. That same year, discrimination was outlawed in post office cafeterias, including the one at Fayette and Calvert Streets, and Black workers were no longer barred from the cafeterias or forced to sit in segregated sections.

Emily Orchard, one of the first Black women enrolled at the University of Maryland Law School, was a 1930 graduate of Frederick Douglass High School, a 1934 graduate of Morgan College, and received a sociology degree from the University of Pennsylvania. She was a social worker and attended law school at night. Although she did not graduate, her admission paved the way for Juanita Jackson Mitchell to become the first Black woman to obtain a degree from the law school in 1950. This 1933 Morgan College report card is for Alonzo Bennett, who was a classmate of Orchard.

Mrs. Amanda Bennett

MORGAN COLLEGE

REPORT OF Bennett, Alonzo   Senior   YEAR

ADDRESS 2312 McCulloh Street,   2nd SEMESTER 19 32 19 33

COURSE TITLE	NO.	SUBJECT TITLE	HRS. PER WEEK	NO. ABSENCES	GRADE	SEMESTER CREDITS
History	10	Eng. Constitutional	3	5	80	3
Mathematics	17	Field Work	2	not in course		
Education	25	Meths. in Math.	1	1	90	1
"	53	Practice Teaching	2	1	78	2
English	28	Playwriting	2	7	82	2
History	3	Seminar - European Hist.	3	4	82	3
Education	22	Teaching Hist. & Civics	1	2	80	1

(over)   Edw. N. Wilson   Registrar

Marion Jackson Downs was the daughter of longtime Baltimore NAACP president Lillie Carroll Jackson. Downs was a talented singer who performed across the country. She was one of the first Black women to be a Fulbright Scholar, and she studied in Milan, Italy. She was noted for largely singing compositions by Black composers such as Samuel Coleridge-Taylor.

Rev. Arthur Jerome Payne was the longtime pastor of Enon Baptist Church. In 1946, Payne unsuccessfully ran for city councilman as a Republican and hoped to encourage other Blacks to enter politics. He was endorsed by Marse Callaway, real estate broker and Black Republican leader; Rev. Baxter L. Matthews, pastor of Union Baptist Church; and Rev. J. Timothy Boddie, pastor of Shiloh Baptist Church.

Five

AFTER *BROWN* V. *BOARD* OF *EDUCATION* 1955–1968

After the Supreme Court ruled that school segregation was unconstitutional in the 1954 *Brown v. Board of Education* decision, Baltimore's journey to desegregation was complex. While some schools, like Polytechnic High School, were integrated prior to *Brown*, others were slow to integrate due to backlash from white parents, staff, and students. The first Black students at formerly all-white schools faced harassment and threats and were often ignored by their peers and teachers. Some also suffered psychological and emotional distress from their experiences.

Although schools were on the path to desegregation, restaurants, department stores, and other public establishments refused to budge. This inspired an interracial movement of high school and college students, including those from Dunbar High School and Morgan State College, along with ministers from across the city to stage sit-ins at Hooper's Restaurant, the Double T Diner, and the White Coffee Pot, to name a few. While they faced harassment and physical harm and were often arrested, they persevered until the restaurants were forced to drop their Jim Crow policies.

The 1950s and 1960s brought in a new crop of politicians and social activists. After almost 25 years of no Black representation on the Baltimore City Council, Walter Thomas Dixon Sr. was elected on a ticket handpicked by white political boss James H. "Jack" Pollack. Dixon's election signified a new direction for the Monumental City's growing Black political base.

Black women were not exempt from this change, as Juanita Jackson Mitchell, Elaine Davis, and Lena King Lee became the first three Black women to get law degrees in Maryland. Lee, Verda Welcome, and Victorine Adams broke barriers on the Baltimore City Council and in the Maryland General Assembly with their elections to political office.

However, the 1968 assassination of Rev. Dr. Martin Luther King Jr. stonewalled Baltimore's progress. As riots broke out across the city and the National Guard was called in, it left ministers, politicians, and community leaders wondering how to move forward.

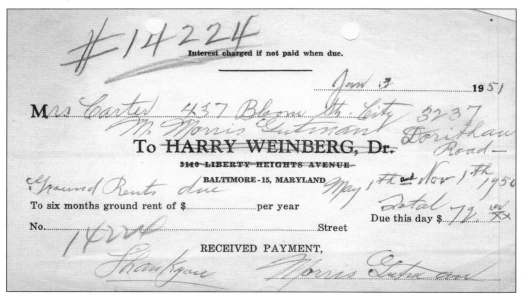

 # 14224

Interest charged if not paid when due.

Jan 3. 1951

M rs. Carter 457 Bloom St. City 3237
M. Morris Gutman Doridau
Road —

To HARRY WEINBERG, Dr.

3140 LIBERTY HEIGHTS AVENUE

BALTIMORE-15, MARYLAND   May 1 Ft and Nov 1 th 1956

Ground Rents due

To six months ground rent of $............per year   Total 72 00 xx

No............   Street   Due this day $......72 00 xx

RECEIVED PAYMENT,

This 1951 ground rent from Harry Weinberg was for Nannie Carter at 437 Bloom Street, which is pictured here. Ground rents were a condition in which a person owned their home, but someone else owned the land upon which the house sat. If a homeowner failed to pay the ground rent, they could lose their home; many Black families became victim to this scheme. In 1968, the Real Estate Brokers of Baltimore, a Black organization, petitioned for ground rents to either be abolished or for land owners to pay the taxes instead of forcing homeowners to pay taxes for land they did not own.

In 1952, Lena King Lee became the third Black woman to receive a law degree from the University of Maryland School of Law. In 1966, she was the first Black woman elected to the Maryland General Assembly, where she served for 16 years. She advocated for teachers' rights, women's rights, and affordable housing. In 1970, she helped to establish the Legislative Black Caucus of Maryland. In this January 1957 letter, Lee thanked Councilman Walter T. Dixon Sr. for his letter to Mayor Thomas D'Alesandro Jr., who appointed Lee to the Baltimore Housing and Urban Renewal Commission, where she fought for affordable housing for the city's Black community.

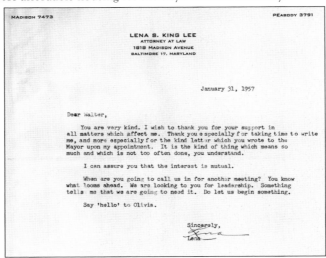

In 1955, Walter T. Dixon Sr. was elected to Baltimore City Council after 24 years of no Black representation on the council. In 1958, he sponsored a bill that barred Baltimore hotels from denying accommodations to Blacks.

```
=LDCO18    PD=BALTIMORE MD 18 NFT=                  1955 OCT 18             06

WALTER K DIXON=

        1208 EUTAW PL BALTO=

1200 CITIZENS AT NAACP MEMBERSHIP MEETING AT SHARPE

STREET MEMORIAL METHODIST CHURCH DOLPHIN AND ETTING

STREET UNANIMOUSLY VOTED TO RESPECTIVELY URGE YOU TO

VOTE AND WORK FOR THE PASSAGE OF FEPC IN THIS CITY

COUNCIL=

        MRS LILLIE M JACKSON PRESIDENT NAACP 402 DOLPHIN ST=
```

Lillie Carroll Jackson, president of the Baltimore NAACP for over 30 years, was the longest-serving Black woman to hold that position. During her tenure, she helped to secure equal pay for Black teachers and supported the 1933 Buy Where You Can Work campaign. In this 1955 telegram to Baltimore City Council member Walter T. Dixon Sr., Jackson urged him to vote for the Fair Employment Practices Committee, which prevented discrimination against Blacks in defense and government jobs—an action Dixon took.

In this August 1956 letter, Dr. Louis V. Blum, noted Jewish doctor, thanked Councilman Walter T. Dixon Sr. for the invitation to speak to the Frontiers Club (pictured below in 1946), a Black service organization. Blum was disappointed that the group rejected his views on the need for segregated housing. In the letter, Blum states, "I insist that the Negro, like any other person, has a right to live where and how he wants to, but he can only do so as long as he does not impose upon the rights of other citizens." He ended the letter with: "Integration with minimal harm, not ghettoization to cause general alarm."

LOUIS V. BLUM, M.D.
2310 Eutaw Place
Baltimore 17, Maryland

August 22, 1956

Mr. Walter T. Dixon
1933 McCulloh St.
Baltimore, Md.

Dear Mr. Dixon:

I thought you would be interested in this article because of what I have been trying to get across to you and to others.

This article says many important things, but what I would like to emphasize again is what I apparently don't seem to put across in my own language.- that is, that population shifts are not only necessary and unavoidable, but are indeed desirable in order to give everyone a chance to live as he wishes; but, at the same time, shifts create problems. I say that this should be recognized by leaders in the community who are closest to the problem and should be tackled with the idea of minimizing the ill effects while affecting maximum benefits for all. I further say that the negro leadership should be in the forefront of organizing all relevant community facilities towards this purpose.

The motto should be: "Integration with minimum harm; not ghettoization creating a general alarm."

Sincerely yours,

Louis V. Blum, M. D.

LVB/gp
Copy to Mr. Samuel T. Daniels

BALTIMORE CHAPTER- FRONTIERS CLUB- 1946.

QUESTIONS AND ANSWERS

REGARDING

Equal Employment Opportunity (FEPC) Ordinance

No. 1839

———••———

THE AMERICAN FEDERATION OF LABOR

THE C. I. O.

THE CATHOLIC INTERRACIAL COUNCIL

THE URBAN LEAGUE

THE BALTIMORE JEWISH COUNCIL

THE DEPARTMENT OF CHRISTIAN SOCIAL
RELATIONS OF THE COUNCIL OF CHURCHES

and

THE NATIONAL ASS'N. FOR THE
ADVANCEMENT OF COLORED PEOPLE

invite your participation
in behalf of
this historic legislation now pending
before the City Council

In 1955, an interracial and interfaith coalition came together to advocate for the passage of the Fair Employment Practices Committee in Baltimore. The groups included the Baltimore Urban League, Baltimore Jewish Council, Catholic Interracial Council, American Federation of Labor, and NAACP. In this pamphlet, the coalition urged other organizations to pass resolutions supporting the ordinance and asked their local council members to vote for the law.

Attorney E. Everett Lane was appointed as the first Black associate traffic court magistrate by Baltimore mayor Theodore McKeldin in 1955. In January 1957, Lane was selected as the first Black judge of the People's Court. Lane was recommended by the Bar Association of Baltimore and the Monumental City Bar Association. He was the son of George M. Lane, one of the first Blacks admitted to the Maryland Bar and reportedly the first Black man to run for mayor of Baltimore.

E. EVERETT LANE

ATTORNEY AT LAW

1607 DIVISION STREET

BALTIMORE, MD.

—

LAFAYETTE 2856

In 1956, an interracial group of 45 people staged a sit-in at the White Coffee Pot Restaurant, led by city council member Walter T. Dixon Sr., pictured in these two images wearing a hat and tie. The protests were designed to show the owners of the restaurant that their discriminatory practices against Black diners was wrong. In September 1958, the Congress on Racial Equality (CORE) staged a sit-in for 10 hours and were refused service. A group picketed outside the restaurant and chanted, "Let's not buy where we all can't eat." They also handed out leaflets to passersby, urging them not to eat at the restaurant until they served all patrons regardless of race.

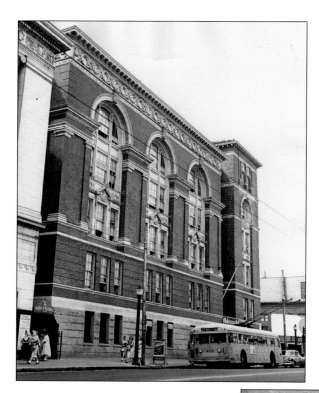

Western High School is one of the oldest all-girls public high schools in the country. In 1954, shortly after the *Brown v. Board of Education* decision, the first group of young Black women integrated the formerly all-white school. Students described the atmosphere created by teachers and staff as "unwelcome." Eva Scott, the first Black teacher assigned to the school, was initially told by the principal that she was not wanted there.

The Black students in this 1958 yearbook were part of the early days of integration at Southern High School. Seventeen days after the 1954 *Brown v. The Board of Education* Supreme Court decision, the Baltimore school board voted unanimously to end segregation in all public schools. When the first Black students showed up for class, white protesters jeered and spat at them and called them derogatory names.

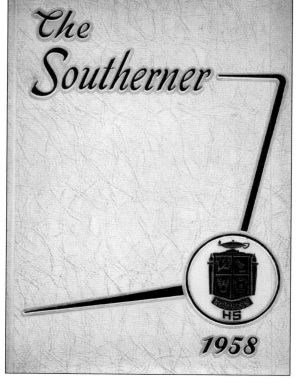

Enolia Pettigen McMillan, an educator for over 42 years, was an advocate for equal pay for Black teachers and better schools for Black children. In 1954, McMillan was one of two Black teachers assigned to the formerly all-white Gen. Robert E. Lee Junior High School in South Baltimore after the Supreme Court outlawed school segregation in the landmark case *Brown v. Board of Education*.

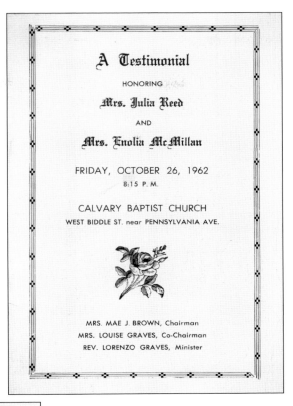

A Testimonial

HONORING

Mrs. Julia Reed

AND

Mrs. Enolia McMillan

FRIDAY, OCTOBER 26, 1962
8:15 P. M.

CALVARY BAPTIST CHURCH
WEST BIDDLE ST. near PENNSYLVANIA AVE.

MRS. MAE J. BROWN, Chairman
MRS. LOUISE GRAVES, Co-Chairman
REV. LORENZO GRAVES, Minister

Brown Memorial Church
BALTIMORE-17, MD.

THE CHURCH HOUSE   1316 PARK AVENUE

January 16, 1957

My dear Mr. Dixon:

Thank you for your letter of January 13th enclosing copies of the letters you have written to others about the possibility of transforming a part of the cemetary around the Knox Community Center into a playground. I feel sure that with your good influence and the help you can secure from others, we shall reach this goal. Thank you again.

Yours very sincerely,

Guthrie Speers

Councilman Walter T. Dixon
1208 Eutaw Place
Baltimore 17, Maryland

Dr. Thomas Guthrie Speers Sr. was a white civil rights activist and a longtime pastor of Brown Memorial Presbyterian Church. Dr. Speers advocated for the passage of legislation to overturn segregation laws in housing, public accommodations, and transportation. He held several interracial conferences at his church that were attended by clergymen, councilmen, and community leaders to discuss race relations. In this January 1957 letter, Speers thanked Councilman Walter Dixon Sr. for his support of the creation of a neighborhood playground.

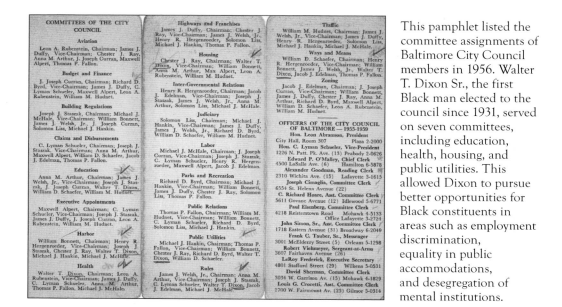

This pamphlet listed the committee assignments of Baltimore City Council members in 1956. Walter T. Dixon Sr., the first Black man elected to the council since 1931, served on seven committees, including education, health, housing, and public utilities. This allowed Dixon to pursue better opportunities for Black constituents in areas such as employment discrimination, equality in public accommodations, and desegregation of mental institutions.

IOTA CHAPTER
CHI DELTA MU FRATERNITY

INVITES YOU TO ATTEND ITS

PUBLIC MEETING of the GRAND CONCLAVE

MONDAY, APRIL 22, 1957 - 8 P.M.

SHARP STREET MEMORIAL METHODIST CHURCH

DOLPHIN AND ETTING STREETS   **BALTIMORE, MARYLAND**

GUEST SPEAKER: DR. D. W. O. HOLMES

AWARDS WILL BE PRESENTED TO:
GOVERNOR THEODORE R. McKELDIN
DOCTOR MORDECAI JOHNSON
MATTHEW R. HADLEY, M.D.

ADMISSION FREE

(GUEST SOLOISTS AND ORGAN MUSIC)

Chi Delta Mu was a Black medical fraternity for the country's prominent doctors, dentists, and others in medical-related professions. This April 1957 invitation for the Baltimore Iota Chapter's meeting was for Councilman Walter T. Dixon Sr. The guest speaker was Dr. Dwight Oliver Wendell Holmes, Morgan State College's first Black president. Awards were presented to Baltimore's mayor Theodore R. McKeldin, an advocate for civil rights, and Dr. Mordecai W. Johnson, the first Black president of Howard University.

This January 1958 flier invited residents to a voting registration rally during which Walter Thomas Dixon Sr., pioneering Baltimore City Council member, and Clarence M. Mitchell Jr., director of the Washington, DC, NAACP Bureau, delivered powerful messages. Dixon discussed discriminatory practices at local hotels, and Mitchell urged Dixon to not attend political events at these hotels until the color line was removed.

HOW CAN YOU HELP END SEGREGATION IN BALTIMORE **?**

COME OUT AND MEET YOUR REPRESENTATIVES at the

2nd DIST. EAST BALTIMORE

MASS MEETING

OF VOTERS AND NON-VOTERS

Wednesday Nite, January 29th
AT 8:00 P. M.

FAITH BAPTIST CHURCH
Bond Street & Ashland Avenue

GUEST SPEAKERS:

CLARENCE M. MITCHELL, JR.
DIRECTOR OF WASHINGTON, D. C. BUREAU OF NAACP

WALTER T. DIXON,
COUNCILMAN 4th DISTRICT — AUTHOR OF CIVIL RIGHTS BILL

Also, All Councilmen, Legislators and Representatives of the 2nd District Invited to Attend

SPECIAL MUSIC: HOLLIMAN STUDENT ORCHESTRA
THE KNOX JEWELS of Knox Presbyterian Church
Also - Mt. Pleasant Baptist Church Choir

ADMISSION FREE
— COME AND BRING YOUR FRIENDS —

Under Sponsorship of NAACP Register & Vote Committee
REV. JOHN L. TILLEY, Chairman
The NAACP Civil Rights Committee
REV. MARCUS G. WOOD, Chairman
MRS. LILLIE M. JACKSON, President

In March 1958, Morgan State College celebrated its second annual Women's Week. The women on this panel discussed the increased opportunities for Black women and the value of a college education. Juanita Jackson Mitchell (first on the left) spoke about how she was encouraged to enter law by the late Charles Hamilton Houston and how her legal career had impacted race relations. Violet Hill Whyte (third from the right), the first Black female police officer, encouraged Black women to get into law enforcement.

Dr. Ruth Wright Hayre (standing at the microphone) was an educator from Philadelphia, Pennsylvania, and the first Black woman principal in that city's school district. Dr. Hayre spoke at the 1958 Women's Week dinner at Morgan State College. She encouraged women to have pride in their heritage and ensure that future generations carried on that legacy. Elizabeth Jenkins, wife of Martin D. Jenkins (then the president of Morgan State College), is seated at left.

Roberta Church (standing) was the daughter of Robert Reed Church Jr., a prominent businessman and political organizer from Memphis, Tennessee. Roberta's grandfather, Robert Reed Church Sr., founded Memphis's first Black bank. During the 1958 Women's Week at Morgan State College, Church spoke about her role as the minority groups consultant in the Department of Labor. Her position required her to negotiate with employers about fair wages and employment practices for Black workers.

The Institute for Political Education, founded in 1959, was a civics program sponsored by Morgan State College designed to educate Morgan State students on political issues and how local laws affected their communities. The program consisted of lectures, seminars, and informal discussion and had a laboratory with voting machines, political maps, televisions, and radios to heighten the students' political awareness. The institute also trained students to work as campaign managers for student elections.

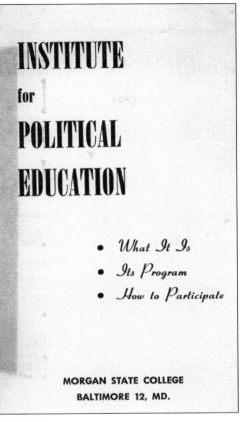

INSTITUTE
for
POLITICAL
EDUCATION

- *What It Is*
- *Its Program*
- *How to Participate*

**MORGAN STATE COLLEGE
BALTIMORE 12, MD.**

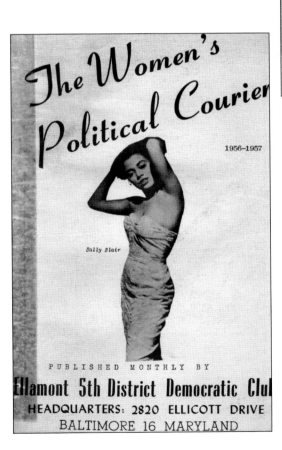

The Women's Political Courier

1956–1957

Sally Blair

PUBLISHED MONTHLY BY

Ellamont 5th District Democratic Club
HEADQUARTERS: 2820 ELLICOTT DRIVE
BALTIMORE 16 MARYLAND

This 1956–1957 issue of the *Women's Political Courier*, with entertainer Sallie Blair on the cover, was published by the Ellamont 5th District Democratic Club, with headquarters located at 2820 Ellicott Drive. The pamphlet kept women abreast of political issues and candidates running for office and encouraged them to support civil rights cases.

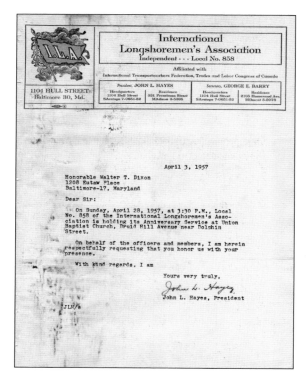

The International Longshoremen's Association (ILA) Local 858 was formed by Black Baltimore dock workers who were denied admission to the all-white Local 829. The union negotiated higher wages for workers. The men of the union regularly contributed to the NAACP and held activities at various Black churches. In this 1957 letter, John L. Hayes, the president of the ILA, invited Councilman Walter T. Dixon Sr. to the Local 858's anniversary service at Union Baptist Church.

Manning-Shaw Realty Inc., located at 1821 Eutaw Place, was co-owned by a Jewish man, Manuel Bernstein, and a Black man, Warren C. Shaw. In an April 4, 1959, article in the *Afro-American*, Shaw advocated for more "block breaking"—Blacks moving into predominantly white blocks, which his company helped them to do.

Nick Aaron Ford was a writer, educator, scholar, and a pioneer of Black literary criticism. In 1945, Ford accepted a professorship at Morgan State College, where he advocated for an African American studies course that explored the impact of African American culture and literature on academics. He believed that Black studies was an academic discipline and that Black colleges, like Morgan State, needed to include more works by Black authors in their courses. In 1950, he completed his second book, *Best Short Stories by Afro-American Writers*, which he coauthored with fellow Morgan State professor Harry Lee Faggett. Ford was very active in his community—he was a member of Enon Baptist Church and chairman of the Christian Board of Education.

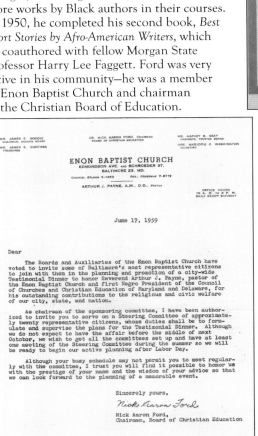

June 17, 1959

Dear

The Boards and Auxiliaries of the Enon Baptist Church have voted to invite some of Baltimore's most representative citizens to join with them in the planning and promotion of a city-wide Testimonial Dinner to honor Reverend Arthur J. Payne, pastor of the Enon Baptist Church and first Negro President of the Council of Churches and Christian Education of Maryland and Delaware, for his outstanding contributions to the religious and civic welfare of our city, state, and nation.

As chairman of the sponsoring committee, I have been authorized to invite you to serve on a Steering Committee of approximately twenty representative citizens, whose duties shall be to formulate and supervise the plans for the Testimonial Dinner. Although we do not expect to have the affair before the middle of next October, we wish to get all the committees set up and have at least one meeting of the Steering Committee during the summer so we will be ready to begin our active planning after Labor Day.

Although your busy schedule may not permit you to meet regularly with the committee, I trust you will find it possible to honor us with the prestige of your name and the wisdom of your advice so that we can look forward to the planning of a memorable event.

Sincerely yours,

Nick Aaron Ford

Nick Aaron Ford,
Chairman, Board of Christian Education

DOES THE U.S. CONSTITUTION APPLY IN MARYLAND

The Civic Interest Group (CIG) was organized in March 1960 by Ronald Merriweather, a group from Morgan State College, and local high school students. They used nonviolent tactics—such as picketing, sit-ins, and negotiations—to integrate public restaurants and department stores. They were often joined by several Black ministers, including Revs. Arthur J. Payne and Marcus Garvey Wood. For several years, Morgan State students had protested at the nearby Northwood Shopping Center and successfully ended segregation at the lunch counters there. They also demonstrated at several Baltimore businesses, including Tommy Tucker's in Edmondson Village and the Hecht Department Stores. Although they were insulted and criticized by restaurant officials and arrested, their efforts resulted in more than 100 facilities removing Jim Crow policies. The CIG office was at 1206 Etting Street, also known as the Sharp Street Community House.

THE CIVIC INTEREST GROUP

cordially invites you to attend

A Banquet

given at

THE MORGAN COLLEGE CANTEEN

ON WEDNESDAY, APRIL 27th, 1960

at 7:30 p. m.

The Civic Interest Group tried to eradicate discrimination at establishments along Route 40, including the Double T Diner. When they were arrested for trespassing at the restaurant, they were bailed out by Rev. Marion Bascom, pastor of Douglas Memorial Church, and were represented in court by Juanita Jackson Mitchell. This 1960 invitation was for a CIG banquet at the Morgan College Canteen.

In 1961, Rev. Dr. I. Logan Kearse, pastor of Cornerstone Baptist Church and a close friend of Rev. Dr. Martin Luther King Jr., led a demonstration at Hooper's Restaurant. Kearse, along with Rev. George A. Crawley Jr., pastor of St. Paul Baptist Church, and Warren Shaw, president of the interracial Manning-Shaw Realty Inc., were arrested. They were charged with trespassing and taken to the Central Police Station, where their bail was posted by William B. Dixon, a Black real estate dealer and insurance executive.

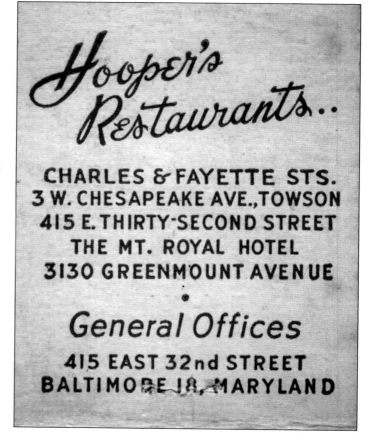

Hooper's Restaurants..

CHARLES & FAYETTE STS.
3 W. CHESAPEAKE AVE., TOWSON
415 E. THIRTY-SECOND STREET
THE MT. ROYAL HOTEL
3130 GREENMOUNT AVENUE
•
General Offices

415 EAST 32nd STREET
BALTIMORE 18, MARYLAND

Vol. XXV, No. 1   DUNBAR JUNIOR HIGH SCHOOL — BALTIMORE 5, MARYLAND   March 3, 1961

THE BROADCAST

BEGIN TODAY
TO MOLD THE YOU
OF TOMORROW

THE SCHOOL'S NEWSPAPER
IS THE SCHOOL'S
STAFF OF LIFE

Sykes, Alston State Views

In order to obtain an inside story of the guest speakers for Student Day, Mr. Lawrence Sykes and Mrs. Fannie Alston were interviewed by Broadcast reporters, Brenda Thompson and Timothy Roberson. Timothy acted as interviewer while Brenda recorded the responses.

An art instructor at Morgan, Mr. Lawrence Sykes, said that he accepted Dunbar's invitation to speak on face value alone. Mrs. Fannie Alston, on the other hand, replied, "My obligation to be of service to the community prompted me to accept your invitation."

Mr. Sykes and Mrs. Alston, who is an instructor of English at Morgan, both had very definite views concerning several phases of school life with particular reference, in several cases, to Dunbar. Their responses were completely natural since both of them are alumni.

When asked if they as students had evern been confronted with a lack of school spirit as that which troubles Dunbar now, they both answered that school spirit, particularly the lack of it, is a universal problem.

"It is a problem mainly because of this fact. A few ultra-active students are spread out to such a

Timothy Roberson checks over final plans for Student Day with committee. From left to right: Hazel Royster, Robert Bell, Brenda Walls, Roland Fletcher, Juanita Swann, Katherine Mooring, Arlene Raymond.

Luther Mitchell Returns As Guest

"It's difficult to express adequately the contributions made by Mr. Luther Mitchell. He has been with us since the organization of the Dunbar Junior High School

tact with many graduates from the first class to the present one. I'm thrilled because we have had thousands of graduates and I've worked with them all."

Students Direct School

Tuesday, March 28, unfolded to the entire student body, administrators, and teachers the dedicated and tedious work of Timothy Roberson and his committee who worked diligently to make Student Day a reality.

This year, the format was essentially the same as that of past Student Days. Included on the agenda were a senior assembly and a luncheon for the Student Council members and their guests. Administrative heads were replaced by Student Council members.

Years '40 to '60 Relived In Play

"Review, " '61--Dunbar Daze" depicts scenes from annual dramatic productions covering a twenty year period, 1940-1960.

Both students and teachers will re-enact these past scenes.

Two performances will be given. The first will be at 3 p.m. Thursday, May 11; the second, 8:15 p.m. Friday, May 12.

The sale of tickets will be under the management of the Future Business Leaders of America, working with all other organizations of the school. Patrons tickets may be purchased for $1.50. Tickets for the evening performance will be sold for $1.00 and matinee tickets for 50 cents.

This procedure marked the first time an assembly program of this nature had been attempted. Formerly, the trend had been to get talent from other schools to come to Dunbar to perform on Student Day. However, a new precedent was established with the participation of teacher talent on Student Day Assembly. Among the talented teachers were Mr. Venable Turner who played the piano and Mr. James Garrett who sang.

Adding to the uniqueness of this Student Day assembly was the fact that former Dunbar students, Mr. Lawrence Sykes, head of the art department at Morgan State College, and Mrs. Fannie Alston, member of the English department at Morgan, were guest speakers on the Student Day program.

This 1961 issue of Dunbar High School's *The Broadcast* features a photograph of Robert Mack Bell (third from left), the plaintiff in the landmark case *Bell v. Maryland*. In June 1960, Bell and a group of students staged a sit-in at Hooper's Restaurant and asked to be served. They were refused service, asked to leave, and then arrested when they did not leave. They were charged with criminal trespassing and fined $10 each. The Baltimore NAACP hired a team of lawyers, including Thurgood Marshall and Juanita Jackson Mitchell, who eventually took the case to the Maryland Court of Appeals, and the students were cleared of charges. Bell attended Morgan State University and Harvard Law School, where he received his JD in 1969. He was a lawyer and judge, and in 1996, he served as the chief judge on the Maryland Court of Appeals, becoming the first Black person to hold the position.

Unveiling of the Portrait
of
Honorable Robert M. Bell
Chief Judge (retired)
Maryland Court of Appeals

The Maryland Courts of Appeal
Annapolis, Maryland
November 7, 2014

Verda Freeman Welcome was elected to the Maryland State Senate in 1962 and was one of the first Black women in the country to hold a state senate seat. During her career, Welcome worked to eliminate Maryland's racial segregation laws, which had been in place since the time of slavery. The Welcome Bridge at Morgan State University is named for her, and her portrait hangs in the James Senate Building in Annapolis, Maryland.

In 1963, Baltimore mayor Theodore R. McKeldin dedicated November 11 through November 17 as NAACP Week. A Freedom Sunday Rally was held at Sharp Street Church on November 17, 1963, at 2:30 p.m. The speaker for the event was Roy Wilkins, executive secretary for the NAACP. During his speech, Wilkins criticized the government's inaction in passing a comprehensive civil rights bill by stating that "Congress has crash programs in everything except civil rights."

Theodore R. McKeldin, who served as Baltimore mayor and Maryland governor, was instrumental in the mid-1960s in the passage of a civil rights bill that ensured equal opportunities in housing, employment, education, and accommodations. The bill was deemed the most sweeping package of civil rights legislation passed at one time. The Theodore R. McKeldin Republican Club advocated for more Black representation throughout Baltimore. In this 1957 letter to Baltimore City Council member Walter T. Dixon Sr., the group wanted more Black representation on the school, jail, and park boards. Emory R. Cole, the president of the club, was an attorney and member of the Monumental City Bar Association. Rev. Ward D. Yerby, the club's secretary, was the former pastor of Perkins Square Baptist Church.

EMORY R. COLE
President
ATTORNEY WILLIAM I. GOSNELL
Vice President
GEORGE DOUGLASS
Treasurer

REVEREND WARD D. YERBY
Secretary
REVEREND ROBERT NEWBOLD
Chaplain

The Theodore R. McKeldin Republican Club

1151 MYRTLE AVENUE
BALTIMORE 1, MD.

January 15, 1957

Councilman Walter Dixon
City Council

Dear Councilman:

The Theodore R. McKeldin Republican Club, in its regular meeting, January 3, 1957, took note of some current situations in our city. We discussed the following:

1. The large percentage of Negros in our schools with only one Negro on the School Board.

2. The large Negro population of our jail and only one Negro on the Jail Board.

3. The increasing Negro population of the city and only one Negro on the Park Board.

The club feels that along with these changes in population in our city that our representation on these above mentioned Boards should be increased. We therefore call this matter to your attention that in the future, if it meets your good pleasure, you might present such recommendation or bill to the Council that would to some extent remedy this situation.

Thanking you in advance for your consideration, we are

Yours for success,

THE THEODORE R. MC KELDIN
REPUBLICAN CLUB
Emory R. Cole, President
Ward D. Yerby, Secretary

MARCH ON WASHINGTON FOR JOBS AND FREEDOM
AUGUST 28, 1963

LINCOLN MEMORIAL PROGRAM

1. The National Anthem	Led by Marian Anderson.
2. Invocation	The Very Rev. Patrick O'Boyle, Archbishop of Washington.
3. Opening Remarks	A. Philip Randolph, Director March on Washington for Jobs and Freedom.
4. Remarks	Dr. Eugene Carson Blake, Stated Clerk, United Presbyterian Church of the U.S.A.; Vice Chairman, Commission on Race Relations of the National Council of Churches of Christ in America.
5. Tribute to Negro Women Fighters for Freedom Daisy Bates Diane Nash Bevel Mrs. Medgar Evers Mrs. Herbert Lee Rosa Parks Gloria Richardson	Mrs. Medgar Evers
6. Remarks	John Lewis, National Chairman, Student Nonviolent Coordinating Committee.
7. Remarks	Walter Reuther, President, United Automobile, Aerospace and Agricultural Implement Workers of America, AFL-CIO; Chairman, Industrial Union Department, AFL-CIO.
8. Remarks	James Farmer, National Director, Congress of Racial Equality.
9. Selection	Eva Jessye Choir
10. Prayer	Rabbi Uri Miller, President Synagogue Council of America.
11. Remarks	Whitney M. Young, Jr., Executive Director, National Urban League.
12. Remarks	Mathew Ahmann, Executive Director, National Catholic Conference for Interracial Justice.
13. Remarks	Roy Wilkins, Executive Secretary, National Association for the Advancement of Colored People.
14. Selection	Miss Mahalia Jackson
15. Remarks	Rabbi Joachim Prinz, President American Jewish Congress.
16. Remarks	The Rev. Dr. Martin Luther King, Jr., President, Southern Christian Leadership Conference.
17. The Pledge	A. Philip Randolph
18. Benediction	Dr. Benjamin E. Mays, President, Morehouse College.

"WE SHALL OVERCOME"

The most iconic civil rights gathering in the history of the United States is the March on Washington, held on August 28, 1963. Thousands flocked to the National Mall in Washington, DC, including a strong contingent of Baltimoreans. There were several pickup locations at historic Black churches, including Metropolitan Methodist Church and St. James Episcopal Church, where participants presented a ticket like the one shown here and boarded the bus to Washington. Baltimore mayor Theodore R. McKeldin delivered a speech at Metropolitan Methodist Church during which he endorsed the Civil Rights Movement. At the march, noted minister and civil rights activist Rev. Dr. Martin Luther King Jr. delivered his famous "I Have A Dream" speech.

NO. 1135

March on Washington

ADMIT 1 ROUND TRIP PASSAGE
Between BALTO. & WASH., D. C.

BUSES LEAVE 7:30 A. M.

WED., AUGUST 28, 1963

Tickets $2.00 Round Trip, Tax Included

NO. 1136

March on Washington

ADMIT 1 ROUND TRIP PASSAGE
Between BALTO. & WASH., D. C.

BUSES LEAVE 7:30 A. M.

WED., AUGUST 28, 1963

Tickets $2.00 Round Trip, Tax Included

Sidney Hollander Sr. was a white businessman and philanthropist who established an award for those who worked to eradicate segregation. Hollander was president of the Baltimore Urban League in the 1940s and served on the board of the National Urban League. He worked for the passage of the 1955 Fair Employment Practices Ordinance. This February 1960 program shows that Hollander received the Stephen S. Wise Medallion for promoting equality and devoting his life to protecting all Americans.

THE MARYLAND STATE COUNCIL
AMERICAN JEWISH CONGRESS

ANNUAL AWARDS BANQUET
presenting the
Stephen S. Wise Medallion
to

MR. SIDNEY HOLLANDER
for devotion to the highest ideals of Judaism in protecting the rights of his fellow Americans

HON. THEODORE R. McKELDIN
as a champion of brotherhood among all faiths, and friend of the State of Israel

TUESDAY, FEBRUARY 16, 1960
6:30 O'CLOCK

BLUE CREST FORDLEIGH
6307 REISTERSTOWN ROAD

The Congress of Racial Equality (CORE), founded in 1942, worked toward equality for all regardless of race. During the 1960s, CORE helped to organize the 1963 March on Washington and the 1964 Freedom Summer, which organized voter registration campaigns in the South. In 1966, the organization launched the Target City Youth Program in East Baltimore, a job-training initiative aimed at eliminating racial discrimination and segregation by providing economic opportunities.

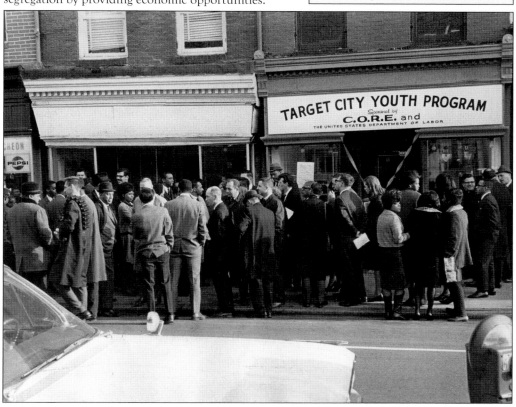

In 1966, the Congress on Racial Equality (CORE), in cooperation with the Humble Oil Company, created a pilot program to train unemployed young Black men in automotive work. The 12-month sessions were held at an Esso Service Station at 900 North Gay Street and consisted of on-the-job training, educational activities, and part-time work. It was part of CORE's Target City Youth Program, an initiative aimed at eliminating racial discrimination and segregation by providing economic opportunities. The two unidentified men shown below, who were employed at the Sinclair Service Station, are examples of those who benefited from this groundbreaking project.

Rep. Parren J. Mitchell (left) is pictured with political and civil rights activist Rev. Jesse Jackson. In their youth, Parren and his brother Clarence participated in civil rights demonstrations. In 1963, Parren Mitchell was appointed as secretary of the Maryland Commissions on Interracial Problems and Relations, where he oversaw the implementation of the state's public accommodation laws. In 1970, Mitchell was elected to the US House of Representatives as the first Black representative from Maryland.

Realtor Daniel W. Spaulding cofounded the Real Estate Brokers of Baltimore and served as its first president. For over 50 years, he fought for the rights of Blacks to purchase homes outside racially-defined boundaries. He used his familial connections to the North Carolina Mutual Life Insurance Company to secure home loans for families. During the 1960s, he lobbied state and federal legislators to pass laws to end discriminatory practices in housing.

Memorial Service
for

Daniel W. Spaulding
October 24, 1909 - July 19, 1999

Saturday, September 11, 1999
11:00 am

Grace Presbyterian Church
2604 Banister Road at Greenspring Avenue
Baltimore, Maryland
Rev. Dr. Arthur St. A. Reynolds, Pastor

A

RECOGNITION DINNER

honoring

DR. MARTIN LUTHER KING, JR.

Winner of the

1964 NOBEL PEACE PRIZE

Sponsored by

CITIZENS OF BALTIMORE

Dr. Logan Kearse, Chairman

Wednesday, March 31st, 1965

THE LORD BALTIMORE HOTEL   BALTIMORE, MARYLAND

8 O'CLOCK

This 1965 recognition dinner was held in honor of Rev. Dr. Martin Luther King Jr., noted pastor, civil rights activist, and winner of the 1964 Nobel Peace Prize. It was sponsored by Rev. Dr. I. Logan Kearse, founder and pastor of Cornerstone Church of Christ. In the 1960s, Kearse was active in Baltimore's civil rights movement and frequently participated in marches and sit-ins. Kearse was a close friend of Dr. King.

First Annual Life Membership

Thanksgiving Freedom Festival

BALLROOM

Sheraton-Belvedere Hotel

CHARLES AND CHASE STREETS

Friday, November 19, 1965

7 P.M.

Baltimore Branch
National Association for the Advancement
of Colored People

COMMEMORATING 30 YEARS OF CONTINUOUS SERVICE
IN THE STRUGGLE TO SECURE JUSTICE AND EQUALITY
FOR ALL MEN.

At the inaugural NAACP Thanksgiving Freedom Festival in 1965, the Baltimore branch outlined their civil rights victories in education, housing, employment, and public accommodations. Some of the people responsible for these victories were seated at the head table, including Baltimore NAACP president Lillie Carroll Jackson, Rev. Arthur J. Payne, Maryland state senator Verda Welcome, Juanita Jackson Mitchell, and judge Robert B. Watts.

In 1966, Baltimore was one of ten cities to receive funding for Operation Champ, a federal initiative aimed at providing children in blighted areas with access to recreational facilities and athletic programs, directed by Olympic and professional athletes, which included players from the Baltimore Bullets basketball team. It operated three "mobile units" which delivered games and playground equipment to neighborhoods across the city, creating pop-up playgrounds. Activities also took place at the Fifth Regiment Armory and were sponsored by the Baltimore City Police Department. The program also established recreational centers inside churches such as St. James Episcopal Church and Ames Methodist Church.

Furman L. Templeton, executive director of the Baltimore Urban League for over 25 years, fought for the rights of Blacks to employment, housing, and education. In the late 1950s, Templeton and five clergymen from the Baltimore Council of Churches challenged discrimination in restaurants and hotels. There is a Baltimore City elementary school named for him.

William B. Henry Sr. (standing) is shown here with the Junior City Council. Henry was a member of the Democratic State Central Committee and active in the East Baltimore political movement. At age 26, he was named Youth Coordinator by Baltimore mayor Thomas D'Alesandro Jr. and placed on the mayor's senior staff. He founded the Baltimore Tutorial Project, which recruited students from Johns Hopkins University, Loyola College (now Loyola University), and others to serve as tutors to East Baltimore youth. He is the father of former councilman and current comptroller William "Bill" Henry II.

Adele Diggs Carr was the daughter of Josiah Diggs, proprietor of East Baltimore's Dunbar Theatre. After Josiah's death in 1938, Carr created the Josiah Diggs Memorial Charity Club to help Black families. At Christmas, the club distributed food to families in need. They also gave blankets to the N.M. Carroll Methodist Home for the Aged, fuel to the Baptist Home for the Colored Aged, and hygiene products to Henryton State Hospital, a tuberculosis institution for Black patients.

Charles "Chuck" Richards was a singer, radio disc jockey, and television personality. He was discovered by a talent manager who heard Richards singing and invited him on a radio program. Richards toured the world with Fletcher Henderson, Mills Blue Ribbon Band, Chick Webb, and other stars. When he returned to Baltimore, he was a disc jockey on WITH, the first white-owned radio station with Black personalities, and on WBAL AM radio. Richards then became the producer and host of *Tomorrow's Stars*, the first regularly sponsored Black television show in Baltimore. Frequent talent on the show included Ethel Ennis, Johnny Sparrow's Band, Erskine Hawkins, and Sonny Till and the Orioles. In the early 1960s, Richards became the first permanent announcer on WCBM AM radio, and in 1964, he joined WMAR TV as an announcer. In this photograph, he is in the back in a dark suit, posing with a class at Booker T. Washington Junior High School.

Wiley E. Daniel Jr. was one of the first Black men to work in television news. He began working at WJZ-TV in 1965 as a general assignment reporter and became an anchorman in 1974, holding that position until his death in 1977. He served as vice president of the Association of Black Media Workers of Baltimore and as an adviser to WEAA-FM, Morgan State University's radio station. This photograph was taken on Christmas Day in 1968. Wiley and his wife, Ruth, are sitting together on the first row.

Today, in church circles, the name Bryant conjures up Jamal Harrison Bryant, pastor of New Birth Missionary Baptist Church in Georgia. However, his church roots run deep; Bryant's grandfather Bishop Harrison John Bryant (pictured here with wife, Edith) pastored several historic AME congregations in Baltimore, including St. John AME and Bethel AME. He was the second-longest-serving pastor at Bethel after Bishop Frank M. Reid III.

Rev. Harold A. Carter, Sr. (first on the right) pastored New Shiloh Baptist Church for almost 50 years. As a civil rights activist, Carter marched with Rev. Dr. Martin Luther King Jr. and was the local coordinator for the 1968 Poor People's Campaign. The church was located at Fremont Avenue and Lanvale Street when this photograph was taken.

This photograph depicts the 1966 groundbreaking of the Arthur J. Payne Christian Center. Payne (fourth from right) pastored Enon Baptist Church for over 40 years, during which time he moved the church to its current location at Edmondson and Schroeder Streets in 1943. George L. Russell Jr. (third from left) was the first Black associate judge of the Baltimore Supreme Bench from 1966 until 1968.

Following the assassination of Rev. Dr. Martin Luther King Jr. in April 1968, riots broke out across the country. Maryland governor Spiro Theodore Agnew called in thousands of National Guard troops and Maryland State Police to quell the riots, and Black ministers pleaded for cooler heads to prevail. At one point, counterprotesters assembled near Patterson Park, but they dispersed after National Guard troops prevented them from entering a Black neighborhood. Over the course of nine days in Baltimore, more than 1,200 small businesses were robbed or destroyed, and the damage was estimated at $12 million. Some Black businesses avoided being looted or destroyed by posting signs like these in the window.

Six

AFTER THE 1968 RIOTS

April 4, 1968, was forever etched into history as a turning point in race relations, because it was the date when Rev. Dr. Martin Luther King Jr. was assassinated. Many Baltimoreans remembered the many visits Dr. King and his wife, Coretta, made to the city's churches, Masonic lodges, schools, houses, and other venues. Decades later, citizens still reflect on Baltimore before the riots and the aftermath.

The city underwent dramatic changes in politics, education, entertainment, and law. After almost 35 years as president of the Baltimore NAACP, Lillie Carroll Jackson was unsuccessful in her reelection campaign against Enolia P. McMillan, an educator and community leader. Jackson's legacy was enshrined in the Lillie Carroll Jackson Civil Rights Museum, which was opened in 1978 by Lillie's daughter Virginia Jackson Kiah and located at Lillie's final residence, 1320 Eutaw Place. This was Baltimore's first privately-owned museum honoring a Black woman. The museum was dormant for years but was reopened in 2016 by Morgan State University.

Victorine Adams—entrepreneur, activist, and wife of William "Little Willie" Adams—made history as the first Black woman elected to the Baltimore City Council in 1968. In the years after 1968, Baltimore also saw its first Black city solicitor, judges, and mayor, along with an increase in Black representation in the Maryland House of Delegates and Senate. In 1970, civil rights activist and state senator Clarence M. Mitchell III and lawyer George L. Russell Jr., the city's first Black solicitor, both ran for mayor. It was the first time in Baltimore's political history that two prominent Black figures ran for mayor at the same time, though neither one was elected.

Morgan State College, one of the city's two historically Black universities and a hub for civil rights activities, changed its name to Morgan State University in 1975, which gave the university access to additional state funding.

Centuries after imposing a ban on interracial marriage, Maryland repealed the law during the start of the *Loving v. Virginia* Supreme Court case in 1967, which allowed mixed couples to get married in 1968.

In 1971, the Royal Theatre, one of Baltimore's iconic entertainment spots, was demolished after operating for over four decades.

Pictured here are the author's parents, George Bayard and Betty Louise Jackson Merrill. The two met while teaching at School No. 16 in Johnston Square. They were married in December 1968, the first year that interracial marriage was legal in Maryland. If they had wanted to get married the prior year, they would have had to do so in Pennsylvania.

George Levi Russell Jr. broke many barriers during his extensive legal career. He was the first Black to serve as Baltimore City solicitor (from 1968 until 1974) and the first Black president of the Bar Association of Baltimore City. He was also the first Black to sit on the Maryland Circuit Court and appellate court. In November 1970, the Baltimore NAACP honored Russell, who was running for mayor, during the group's annual Freedom Dinner.

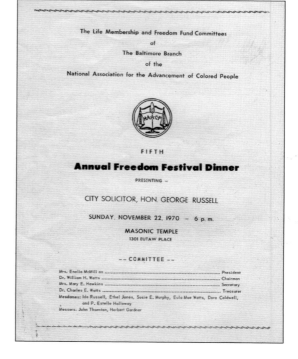

Joseph Clemens Howard Sr. became the first Black to win an election as a judge on the Baltimore City Supreme Bench in 1968. Howard was born in Ohio and moved to Baltimore in 1959, where he established a law practice with his brother Charles and John R. Hargrove Sr., known as Howard & Hargrove. As a judge, Howard challenged the discriminatory hiring practices of the supreme bench and employed more Blacks at the circuit court.

Enolia P. McMillan succeeded Lillie Carroll Jackson as president of the Baltimore NAACP in 1969. Under McMillan's leadership, membership expanded to over 5,000 members, which included over 800 youth. McMillan sought to engage young Black militants who felt that the NAACP was out of touch with the current civil rights movement. This letter, signed by McMillan, was given to the family of Rev. Edmond D. Meade, who passed away in 1985.

Dr. Benjamin Joseph Kimbers Jr. moved to Baltimore in 1952 and established his dental practice at North Avenue and Monroe Street. In 1970, Kimbers joined eight Black medical and dental professionals in developing the Madison Park Medical Center on West North Avenue. It was one of three Black medical centers in Baltimore; the other two were Garwyn Medical Center and Village Medical Center.

Victorine Quille Adams was an educator, entrepreneur, and the first Black woman to serve on the Baltimore City Council. She served four terms, from 1967 to 1983. During her tenure, she established the Baltimore Fuel Fund, a public-private partnership that raised money to provide families with financial assistance for heating costs. The fund was renamed the Victorine Q. Adams Fuel Fund and was replicated in other parts of Maryland.

Milton Burke Allen became Maryland's first Black state's attorney in 1970 and the first Black person to hold a chief prosecutor's position in a major city. He was also a founding partner of Brown, Allen, and Watts, the first major Black law firm in the state. Allen sat on the Baltimore City Supreme Bench from 1976 to 1986. He graduated from Frederick Douglass High School in 1935 and from Coppin Teacher's College in 1938. He served in World War II and used his GI bill benefits to pay his tuition at the University of Maryland Law School. He was admitted to the Maryland Bar in 1948, a year before he completed his law degree.

VOTE FOR

Milton B. ALLEN

FOR

STATES ATTORNEY

TUESDAY, SEPTEMBER 10, 1974

LEVER No. 14A

Authority: Milton B. Allen, Jr., Treas.

Sterling S. Keyes served as the acting Baltimore City School System superintendent in the early 1970s before Dr. Roland N. Patterson was appointed. Keyes was born and raised in New Jersey and was part of the staff for Dr. Thomas D. Sheldon, head of the Hempstead, New Jersey, school system. When Sheldon was appointed superintendent of Baltimore schools in 1968, Keyes was his assistant; he was promoted to interim superintendent when Sheldon resigned. Keyes was the youngest man and first Black to lead the city's school system, and he held the position for six months. When Dr. Patterson was appointed as superintendent, Keyes was reassigned to assistant superintendent. The 1971 Northwestern High School diploma below is signed by Keyes.

Northwestern High School

BY AUTHORITY OF THE STATE OF MARYLAND
VESTED IN THE BOARD OF SCHOOL COMMISSIONERS UNDER PROVISIONS
OF THE CHARTER OF THE CITY OF BALTIMORE

T H I S

Diploma

has been awarded to

OSSAREW FISKE GEE III

UPON THE SUCCESSFUL COMPLETION OF THE

COLLEGE PREPARATORY CURRICULUM

Given under our hands and the seal of the City this _____tenth_____ *day*
of _____June_____ *, 19* 71

Edward L. Goldsmith
PRINCIPAL

Robert L. Hammel
PRESIDENT OF BOARD OF SCHOOL COMMISSIONERS

Thomas J. D'Alesandro III
MAYOR

Sterling S. Keyes
ACTING SUPERINTENDENT OF PUBLIC INSTRUCTION

Dr. Roland Nathaniel Patterson was appointed the first Black permanent superintendent of the Baltimore City School System in 1971. Under Patterson's leadership, the school system was reorganized, and several educational programs were initiated to help Black Baltimore youth, including the Gifted and Talented program. Patterson's colleagues credited him as laying the groundwork for improved test scores and parental involvement. In this photograph, he is shaking hands with Baltimore mayor William Donald Schaefer (right).

Dr. Roland N. Patterson (second from right) is pictured with his wife, Marian, at a reception celebrating his appointment as superintendent of the Baltimore City School System. He was elected to the position by a vote of 8–1 by the Board of School Commissioners. Patterson's career in education administration began in 1960, when he served as both a principal and superintendent in New Jersey and Washington schools. His arrival in Baltimore in 1971 was hailed by the *Afro-American* newspaper as a "breath of fresh air."

Dr. Roland N. Patterson, shown here with three unidentified children, instituted various innovative and creative programs. In addition to the Right to Read and the Gifted and Talented program, he created Parent Infant Centers, the Office of Student Relations, and the Office of Staff Development. Patterson involved students, teachers, staff, and the community in the reorganization of the Baltimore school system.

The National Right to Read Program of the Baltimore City Public Schools

This Certificate is awarded to

PATTIE HOLLOWAY

of

SARAH M. ROACH SCHOOL 73

for successfully completing a three-day training period in the Right to Read Program during the school year 1972-73.

Dorothy Clayborne
Project Manager, Right to Read

Marie S. Francis
Assistant Project Manager, Right to Read

6-19-73
Date

Roland N. Patterson
Roland N. Patterson, Superintendent

Bernice S. Turner
Principal

The Right to Read program was initiated in January 1973 by superintendent Dr. Roland N. Patterson in an effort to improve literacy in schools. It was supported by Baltimore mayor William Donald Schaefer, who proclaimed every September as Right to Read Month. The program consisted of three-day workshops for teachers and increased reading instruction in the classroom. This certificate was awarded to Pattie Holloway, teacher at Sarah M. Roach School No. 73, who completed the workshop.

Parren James Mitchell was elected the first Black US representative from Maryland in 1970. Mitchell's civil rights activism began in his youth, when he and his brother Clarence participated in demonstrations against segregation in the 1940s and 1950s. During his legislative career, Mitchell focused on passing a series of bills that promoted minority-owned businesses and small firms. In 1976, he attached an amendment to a $4 billion public works program that required state and local governments applying for federal contracts to reserve 10 percent of this money for minority-owned companies. Mitchell later described this effort as his proudest congressional accomplishment.

Clarence M. Mitchell III was part of a political dynasty. His father, Clarence M. Mitchell Jr., was an NAACP lobbyist known as the "101st US Senator" for his efforts in securing the passage of civil rights legislation. His mother, Juanita Jackson Mitchell, was the first Black woman to earn a law degree from the University of Maryland School of Law and represented plaintiffs in several civil rights cases. This campaign card of Mitchell (left) and Pres. Lyndon B. Johnson encouraged citizens to vote for Mitchell for state senator. In 1963, Mitchell was elected to the Maryland House of Delegates at age 22, and in 1967, he ran for the Maryland State Senate and won. The card outlined Mitchell's victories as a delegate, including the passage of a law against Ku Klux Klan crosses and his fight to increase the minimum wage.

In 1970, future councilman Norman V.A. Reeves, Roosevelt Duncan, and Howard P. Rawlings called for the formation of a Black legislative caucus. Their efforts came to fruition later that year, when the Maryland Black Legislative Caucus was incorporated by Delegate Lena K. Lee. The mission of the caucus was to examine all bills that affected Maryland's Black population. Reeves was also an advocate of celebrating Black history; in 1968, he urged Baltimore mayor Thomas D'Alesandro III to proclaim the second week of February as Afro-American History Week in the city. Reeves believed it would highlight the significant contributions that Blacks had made to the country. Reeves was elected to the Baltimore City Council in 1979. When he died in 1983, his wife, Iris, was selected to fill his council seat.

Maj. James H. Watkins was the second-highest-ranking Black officer in the Baltimore Police Department. Watkins joined the police force in 1951 and was assigned to foot patrol in the Northwestern District. He also held positions in the Northern District, Criminal Investigation Division, Inspectional Services, and Tactical Squad. In 1971, then-commissioner Donald D. Pomerleau named him a major, and four years later, Watkins became a lieutenant colonel.

Clarence W. Blount was the first Black majority leader of the Maryland State Senate. Before entering politics, Blount was an educator and principal at Dunbar High School and an executive assistant to the president of Community College of Baltimore. He was elected to the Maryland State Senate in 1970. In 1983, he was chosen as majority leader, and in 1987, he was selected as the first Black chairman of a Senate committee.

In 1971, Dr. John T. Chissell became the first Black president of the Maryland Academy of Family Physicians. Originally from Virginia, Dr. Chissell moved to Baltimore in 1955 to join his brother Dr. H. Garland Chissell Jr., and they later relocated to the Madison Park Professional Center, a medical office of Black doctors and dentists. When John retired, he advocated for Black patients to consider alternative medicine for conditions such as hypertension.

A Celebration of Life
for

John T. Chissell, M.D.
May 31, 1926—May 20, 2004

Benjamin Carr Whitten was a longtime educator and president of the Baltimore Urban League in the early 1980s. Whitten, who was born in Delaware, came to Baltimore in the 1940s and taught industrial arts at Carver Vocational-Technical High School. In 1968, he was appointed director of vocational education for city schools. During this time, he persuaded Mayor William Donald Schaefer to donate the Hollywood Diner to the city to train vocational students in foodservice careers.

Walter Percival Carter worked for civil rights until the day he died in 1971 at the age of 48. On July 30, 1971, the day before he passed, he won a court battle against realtor Morris Goldseker. Carter led protests outside Goldseker's office, calling on him to stop the Black Tax, which involved excessive rent-to-own fees charged to Black tenants in an effort to scam them out of homeownership. The Walter P. Carter Elementary/Middle School is named for him.

William Rodwell "Bill" Perry Jr. was closely aligned with Walter P. Carter in the civil rights struggle. Perry, the director of the Model Cities Innovation team, worked closely with Betty L. Merrill to provide educators with new ways of teaching. Model Cities was a federally funded program and part of Pres. Lyndon Johnson's Great Society and the War on Poverty. It developed a network of neighborhood councils that served as advocacy and policy centers. Perry later became the director of the Baltimore City school system's first Office of Staff Development.

Henry Green Parks Jr. was an entrepreneur, Baltimore City Council member, and the founder of the Parks Sausage Company, the first Black-owned enterprise to go public on Wall Street. In this letter to voters, Parks encouraged them to endorse the Right On ticket that was headed by State Senator Clarence M. Mitchell III and included Parks, who was running for reelection to the Democratic State Central Committee. The Right On ticket was committed to securing employment, housing, and education for Black Baltimoreans.

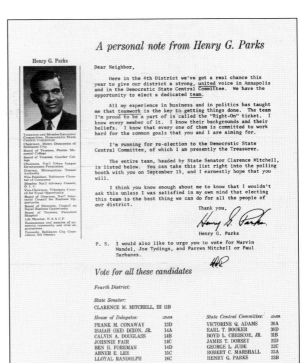

This January 1970 invitation announced the formation of the Metro Democrats, Inc., an organization of Black politicians and community residents. Members included Delegate Lloyal Randolph, the second chairman of the Legislative Black Caucus; George Linwood Jude, the first Black commissioner of the Baltimore City Planning Commission; and Ethel P. Rich, a businesswoman and founder of Women Power, Inc. Rich's group organized voter registration drives, trained census-takers, and taught people how to use voting machines.

YOU AND YOUR FRIENDS
ARE CORDIALLY INVITED
TO ATTEND A

PRESS CONFERENCE

ANNOUNCING THE
ORGANIZATION OF

METRO - DEMOCRATS, INC.

THURSDAY, JANUARY 29, 1970
7 TO 9 P.M.

WILSON'S RESTAURANT
PENNSYLVANIA AND NORTH AVENUES

REFRESHMENTS

In 1977, Rev. Vernon Nathaniel Dobson, the longtime pastor of Union Baptist Church, and two other ministers formed Baltimoreans United in Leadership Development (BUILD). During the group's first few years, it focused on obtaining better police protection for communities, improving housing, and eradicating pests. Dobson was a member of the Goon Squad, a coalition of ministers and lawyers who advocated for civil rights.

BALTIMORE BRANCH N. A. A. C. P.

Annual Human Dolls On Parade For Freedom

DOUGLAS MEMORIAL COMMUNITY CHURCH
Madison and Lafayette Avenues

SUNDAY, JUNE 15, 1975 - 3:30 p. m.

Mrs. Ida Russell, Program Chairman

Mrs. Viola Jackson, General Chrm. Mrs. Eula Mae Watts, Prog. Co-Chrm.
Mrs. Rebecca Brown, Co-Chrm.   Mrs. Susie Murphy, Hostess Chrm.
Mrs. Eliza Costin, Co-Chrm.   Mrs. Enolia P. McMillan, President

This ticket for the 1979 Baltimore NAACP Human Dolls on Parade for Freedom was one of many ways the organization raised funds for its various causes. This was a contest where parents voted for children aged six months to five years, and the child with the most votes won a scholarship and a loving cup.

Rev. Jesse Jackson, the founder of Operation PUSH (People United to Save Humanity) in Chicago, was brought to Baltimore in 1977 to promote the program's Push for Excellence. It was aimed at reforming inner-city schools by engaging teachers, students, and parents in the educational process. It stressed community involvement, greater discipline, and self-empowerment. While there, Jackson was escorted around the school system by Betty L. Merrill, and he signed this pamphlet to the author.

A School System's

Push For Excellence

Baltimore City Public Schools

1977-78

Walter Robert Carr's magazine, *Nitelifer*, served several purposes. It was a directory of Black nightclubs and businesses, and the editorial page was used to urge Blacks to be empowered and take control of their communities. Walter and his wife, Hannah, were ardent civil rights activists. They were arrested on a few occasions for protesting police brutality. This is a November 1971 edition.

Bishop John Richard Bryant, son of Bishop Harrison James and Edith Holland Bryant, was elected and consecrated as the 106th Bishop of the African Methodist Episcopal Church in 1988. When he became pastor of Bethel AME Church, he instituted several community events. For example, he turned the church's traditional Labor Day celebration into an event to help the city's jobless population. He encouraged local employers to bring job offers and clothing donations to the event.

While historic designation for white communities has been common practice for many decades, Black neighborhoods were often overlooked. In this 1978 letter, Milton E. Branch Sr., president of the Madison Avenue Neighborhood Club, expressed his desire for the 2200–2300 blocks of Madison Avenue to be designated as a historic neighborhood. Ultimately, the club was going to send a letter to Mayor William Donald Schaefer and ask him to support the designation. This letter encouraged residents and politicians to lend their assistance to the effort.

MADISON AVENUE NEIGHBORHOOD CLUB
2339 MADISON AVENUE
BALTIMORE, MARYLAND 21217

January 3, 1978

Dear Mrs. Gee_____:

The Residents of the 2200 – 2300 Blocks of Madison Avenue would like for these blocks to be declared a Historical Neighborhood.

We will be sending a letter very soon to Mayor Schaefer expressing our desire to have our Neighborhood designated a Historic District.

On Monday, January 23, 1978, the Madison Avenue Neighborhood Club will meet at 2261 Madison Avenue at 7:30 p.m. Mrs. Hoff from the Mayor's Office on Historic Preservation will be present to explain the program to the members of our organization.

We would like to extend an invitation to you to be present and give any assistance and support for this project.

Sincerely yours,

Milton E. Branch, Sr.
President

MEB:mbw

cc: John Anderson
    Mabel S. Gee
    Congressman Parren J. Mitchell
    Senator Verda Welcome
    Delegate Kenneth L. Webster
    "   Troy F. Brailey
    "   Lloyal Randolph
    Councilwoman Victorine Q. Adams
    "   Mary Pat Clarke
    Councilman Michael B. Mitchell
    Councilman Eberson Julian

Samuel T. Daniels served as Grand Worshipful Master of the Prince Hall Masons for 38 years, from 1960 until 1998. He was the executive director of the Baltimore Council for Equal Business Opportunity, a private organization that encouraged Black participation in business. In 1968, Daniels was appointed to the school board by Mayor Thomas D'Alesandro III, who described Daniels as a calming influence on the board during unsettling times.

Clarence Henry "Du" Burns was the first Black Baltimore City Council president and the city's first Black mayor. He was elected to the city council in 1971 and served as council president from 1982 to 1987. He became mayor in 1987 to fulfill the unexpired term of then-mayor William D. Schaefer, who had been elected governor of Maryland. Some of Burns' mayoral achievements included the creation of the new Dunbar High School complex.

BIBLIOGRAPHY

"Baltimore elects Dixon to Council." *Afro-American*, May 14, 1955.

Breihan, John R., Jessica I. Elfenbein, and Thomas Hollowak, eds. *From Mobtown to Charm City: New Perspectives on Baltimore's Past*. Maryland Historical Society: 2002.

"The Civic Interest Group." The Civil Rights Movement Archive, accessed October 6, 2022. www.crmvet.org/docs/61_cig.pdf.

Halpin, Dennis. *A Brotherhood of Liberty: Black Reconstruction and Its Legacies in Baltimore, 1865–1920*. Philadelphia: University of Pennsylvania Press, 2019.

The Road from Frederick to Thurgood: Black Baltimore in Transition, 1870–1920, Maryland State Archives.

Sharp Street Memorial Methodist Church. "Souvenir Program: One Hundred Fiftieth Anniversary, 1802–1952." Baltimore, MD: 1952.

Skotnes, Andor. *New Deal for All?: Race and Class Struggles in Depression-Era Baltimore*. Durham: Duke University Press, 2012.

Thompson, M. Dion. "Early Who's Who of Black Baltimore Directories: Listings of African-American Doctors, Lawyers and Dentists in 'First Colored' Offer a Glimpse into the First Half of the Century." *Baltimore Sun*, August 23, 1997.

INDEX

Discover Thousands of Local History Books
Featuring Millions of Vintage Images

Arcadia Publishing, the leading local history publisher in the United States, is committed to making history accessible and meaningful through publishing books that celebrate and preserve the heritage of America's people and places.

Find more books like this at
www.arcadiapublishing.com

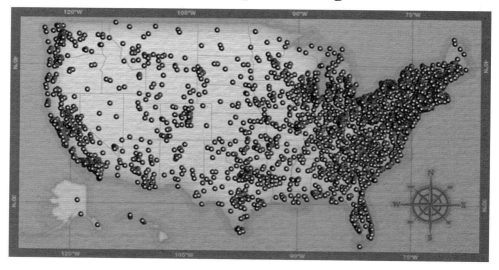

Search for your hometown history, your old stomping grounds, and even your favorite sports team.